COMPLETE GUIDE
TO
TRAINING GUNDOGS

COMPLETE GUIDE
TO
TRAINING GUNDOGS

James Douglas

Photographs by James Douglas
Line illustrations by Ken Hooks

Pelham Books London

First published in Great Britain by
Pelham Books Ltd
44 Bedford Square
London WC1B 3DP
1985

British Library Cataloguing in Publication Data

Douglas, James, 1944–
    Complete guide to training gundogs.
    1. Hunting dogs 2. Dogs—Training
    Rn: Douglas Mitchell   I. Title
    636.7′52   SF428.5

ISBN 0-7207-1629-2

Printed and bound in Great Britain by
Butler & Tanner Ltd, Frome and London

Dedicated to all gundog owners who strive to achieve the highest standards when working with their dogs in the field.

CONTENTS

STANDARDS OF THE BREEDS REPRINTED BY KIND PERMISSION OF THE KENNEL CLUB

ILLUSTRATIONS

DRAWINGS

PHOTOGRAPHS

INTRODUCTION

History does not record when the ancestors of the dog first began to share shelter and food with man. It is known that the Saluki was domesticated as early as 329BC, but dogs certainly lived with men long before that. One can imagine early man sitting in his camp after a meal, with some canine creature hanging around the periphery attracted by the smell of food, and being thrown a bone, perhaps not even as a favour but more as a means of chasing the animal away. The 'dog' would lie down to chew the discarded bone and on hearing the approach of another intruder, whether man or beast, would jump to its feet growling a warning, which the man saw as a useful service.

Or perhaps some hunters had discovered that the early dogs were better suited than humans to catching animals such as deer, and that if they were cunning and followed the dogs until they brought the beast down, they could chase the dogs away and steal the kill. If they were wise, of course, they would throw some of the meat back to the dogs, so as not to discourage them completely.

Whatever the actual beginnings of the relationship were we will probably never know, but it is certain that whatever the circumstances it was an arrangement that suited both man and dog well, and the very special relationship that exists between the two creatures was born. Although there are instances in nature of other pairs of animals providing service to each other, no other two species have developed anything like the unique bond between man and dog. Through the centuries men, with their greater intelligence, have used their relationship with this highly adaptable animal to train him to do many tasks, which with his better senses of sight or hearing, speed or aggression, make him invaluable to his human friends.

Since early times dogs have been used for many tasks and are still used in service as guards, messengers, war dogs, herders of other domesticated animals, life guards, dragging animals, heat sources and food gatherers. Even today, with the highly sophisticated technology available to the armed services and police forces, they are still used, not only to apprehend fugitives, but to sniff out substances secreted by the cleverest criminals. Of course dogs are also used purely as companions. In all parts of the world, no matter how extreme the temperature, dogs are to be found; for wherever men are you will find a dog. We have changed their appearance, with selective breeding, to suit our own needs, yet all they ever ask in return is that we provide them with a home and food. It is little wonder, when you think of how much they mean to us and of the centuries of willing and devoted service and companionship, that they are referred to as 'man's best friend'.

Since hunting in the company of dogs began men have debated what is the best dog for them, to suit their particular type of game and terrain. We have developed dogs with highly specialised abilities and skills and of widely varying sizes, coats and shapes – all in the general pursuit of finding and developing the perfect dog for the job. This book is about the shooting breeds and their different categories – the hunters, the pointers and the retrievers.

I have carefully put together all aspects of the training regime applicable to all breeds of gundog, using everything that is necessary for the retrieving breeds as a basis. The reader needs only to follow carefully the laid down schedule. If you own, or are going to train, a spaniel or any of the Hunting/Pointing/Retrieving (HPR) breeds, then the chapters on quartering or pointing obviously apply to these breeds specifically.

It should be remembered that the basis of all animal training, whether it is a lion performing at the circus, an elephant hauling logs through an Indian forest, or a gundog performing in the field for its handler, is obedience, where the trainer, using kindness and his infinitely greater powers of intelligence, has taught the animal to perform the allotted task. Training of any animal can only be achieved though kindness, love and affection, coupled with firmness. Try to bully your animal or force it to do something which it is not yet prepared for and you will come unstuck. But if you approach it with kindness and understanding, both you and your animal companion will develop a bond which is personal and brings its own rewards.

1. CHOOSING THE RIGHT BREED

The early shotguns were muzzle loaders, used in the main by the wealthy landowners who controlled much of the land and sport, particularly the large moorland areas. Since the muzzle loader was essentially a weapon which took some time to load between shots, and since the majority of shooting was practised on vast open areas, the ideal dogs for the early shotgunner were the pointers and setters. These dogs had been developed for their physical abilities to cover vast areas of land, ranging in front of the gun until they scented game. They then took a set or point, indicating the presence of the game and giving the shooter ample time to make his way to the dog, and when he was ready, flush the game. It was the invention of the breech loader, a much faster method of shooting, that started the decline in popularity and use of the pointers and setters. For the breech loader made it possible for driven shooting to develop, and now a dog that would spring game from cover was required, one that would busy about flushing the game, sending it out and away towards the standing guns. The breech loader also made it less necessary for the shooter to have warning of the game's impending presence. It was now possible for a dog to busy down a hedgerow flushing game in front of his handler, and the spaniels came into their own.

As greater numbers of game were shot, this opened the door for the specialist retrievers who were the stylish experts at finding and picking lost and wounded game. As the sport of shooting continued to increase in popularity across the social spectrum so the types of shooting continued to diversify, with more and more sportsmen specialising in the particular aspect of shooting that took their fancy, whether it be grouse, ground game, or wildfowling. Add to this the personal preferences that individuals had for one breed or another and the future was assured for many breeds of dog.

Whilst British sporting dog enthusiasts continued to strive to produce the highest possible standards in the various different breeds that they themselves most preferred, they never tried to combine the attributes, rather concentrating on keeping their breeds pure. It was the continental shooters who developed the different breeds that were intended to perform all the functions that the three separate categories of dog – hunters, pointers and retrievers – did so well and so the HPR breeds were established.

The idea was obviously a good one– a dog that could do all three jobs. The basic reason that the continentals saw the need for such a dog was that they are likely to encounter a greater range of game in a day than we are in Britain – boar, deer or game birds. And just as they later developed a gun known as a drilling, which was a combination of rifle and shotgun barrels clustered together to accommodate all game, so also did they develop multi-purpose dogs. These were dogs with the versatility to range in front of the hunter, to point and hold game, then to retrieve the game from either land or water.

If the game was large or wounded, the dog was able to track the beast through the dense German forests. The dog was able to keep up a good, fast pace all day, in any terrain and to be everything that the 'jäger' could possibly wish for in a dog.

The continentals also have a different attitude towards field sports. In Britain we developed a tradition of *either* going stalking for stags with a rifle, *or* shooting birds with a shotgun and we have a general national tendency to underplay our sporting activities. The continentals, on the other hand, refer to all shooting as hunting, and there is a general tendency to regard their shooting sport as a more male 'macho' activity. Anyone who has witnessed some of the traditions and ceremonies that surround much of their sporting activities can see that there is a greater emphasis placed on taking the matter very seriously, and a greater appreciation for the quarry than we publicly display in Britain. To be fair however, much of Germany and Hungary is covered with large forests, and a wounded animal could speedily vanish into the dense cover, so a dog that was adept at following a trail obviously had its uses. And if the same dog also had the ability to retrieve a bird from water, then the need for owning two animals was negated.

There are many claims made by dog enthusiasts about the various aspects of the different breeds. Most dog owners tend to think that their breed is supreme. The sensible potential dog owner should carefully decide the type of shooting he does most of, and which dog would best suit his needs and then combine this with the breed he is most attracted to, since I believe a large part of owning and successfully training a gundog is that you like his looks.

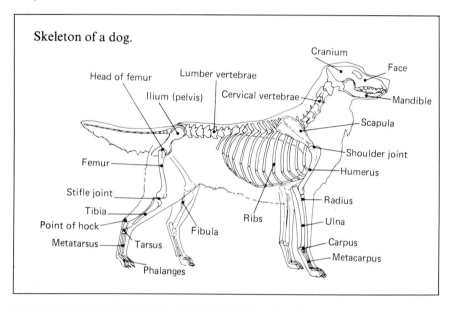

Skeleton of a dog.

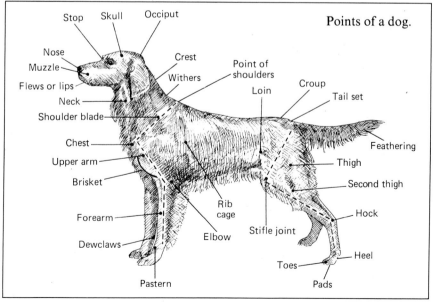

Points of a dog.

RETRIEVERS

CHESAPEAKE BAY RETRIEVER

The origins of the Chesapeake Bay retriever, also known as the American Duck retriever, reads like an episode from a period drama. There are several stories accounting the origins of the breed, and although they all differ slightly, they all tie together with the relevant names and places.

In the early 1880s an English brig set sail from Newfoundland. On board were two Newfoundland puppies, a dog and a bitch. Off the coast of Maryland the ship started to take water and founder, but an American ship, the *Canton*, from the port of Baltimore, rescued both the crew and the two puppies. The dog, which is said to have been a dirty red colour and called 'Sailor', was handed over to a Mr James Mercer of West River; and the bitch, who was said to have a black coat, was given to a Dr James Stewart of Sparrow Point. Both dogs were compact, strongly built animals, although not quite as large as Newfoundland puppies of the same age would have been expected to be. They had medium length coats with thick wavy hair.

There the details of this particular story become sketchy, but the two dogs apparently achieved some considerable local attention in the Chesapeake area as duck dogs, and it is assumed that these two dogs, though there are no records to show that they were ever bred together, were put together with local retrievers and hound stock, from which it is accepted the Chesapeake Bay retriever evolved. Flatcoated and curly-coated retrievers, and the local otter hounds all possibly added their blood to the development of the breed.

However, the version of the story that I prefer and which holds most credibility was recounted by General Ferdinand C Latrobe, a one-time mayor of Baltimore. This story claims that the English vessel unfortunately grounded in the coast waters lying off the Walnut Grove Estate, which is situated on the banks of the Chesapeake River. This estate was the home of a well-known and established New England family, headed by a Mr John Law. As a gesture of gratitude for the help in saving the crew, and the hospitality which they were shown on the estate, the two puppies from the English vessel were presented to John Law as a token of the captain's gratitude and respect. There the puppies remained in the estate kennel and were bred

Chesapeake Bay retriever.

with the local coon hounds. Certainly the introduction of the yellow and tan coloured coon hound, plus the eventual introduction of a great many different water spaniel strains, is the most likely and credible source of many of the Chesapeake's attributes of stamina, scenting power, and of course colouration, which is a yellowy liver colour.

The Chesapeake Bay retriever is an utterly superb and highly specialised water dog. His development has suited him quite perfectly for his environment. The outer coat is highly water resistant, harsh to the touch, tight and distinctly wavy, with an undercoat of a soft dense oily consistency, which gives the coat an almost total water resistance. In company with the labrador, the Chesapeake shares the distinction of being one of the two dogs most popularly used by the American market gunners of the east coast of America. Unfortunately the Chesapeake is not common in Europe, and the chances of any British field sportsman managing to find top-class working Chesapeakes are very remote.

LABRADOR RETRIEVER

For good reason the Labrador retriever is the most popular

and widely accepted retrieving dog in Britain, for this breed is truly the master of all forms of retrieving, whether in the high grouse moor or fowling in the harsh coastal areas.

Originally referred to as the St John's breed from Newfoundland, the breed was probably brought to Britain during the nineteenth century aboard ships trading from the north-eastern seaboard, particularly from Newfoundland and the Labrador coasts. These vessels landed their cargoes on the west coast ports of Britain, including the Clyde in Scotland and Poole in Dorset. When one understands the highly privileged society of the nineteenth century, when the landed gentry spent much of their time in the pursuit of game and all things sporting, it is easy to understand how these breeds found their way into the hands of the noble families.

Labrador sitting with greylag goose.

The second Earl of Malmesbury, who had an estate near Poole, is known to have acquired a dog which was taken to work on his sporting estate. So impressed was he by the dog's general abilities as a field sports dog, that the family bought other specimens of the breed and set up their own small population at the estate kennel keeping the breed as pure as possible. It was the third Earl who referred to the breed as his labradors.

The Dukes of Hamilton, Buccleuch, and the Earl of Home all had estates in the region of Scotland to the south of the Clyde, and it is most likely that some of the labradors that appeared in their kennels originated from these sea traders, although it is known that they also received dogs into their Scottish stock from the Malmesbury kennel. Other personalities such as the Honorable A Holland-Hibbert, later to become Lord Knutsford, did much to establish the breed, and of course the Royal Family took numbers of the breed into their kennels. Such an accolade, combined with the brilliance of his work, assured the breed's future.

Labrador retriever.

However, no mention of the labrador breed can ever be made without acknowledging the efforts of Lorna, Countess Howe, who probably did more than anyone else to establish the labrador. It was she who founded the first breed club, and she is largely responsible for the compilation and setting down of the breed standard.

The labrador is probably the dog that holds the distinction
of being used as a water dog for the longest period of time, for
he was the master of the cold, wild waters from the region in
which he developed in the communities around Newfoundland
– communities that made much of their living from the seas
and the river estuaries. The labrador was used as a general
factotum on the fishing boats when they set out to long line the
cod. It was he who was asked to pick ropes that may have
fallen over the side, to take messages from one boat to another,
or, holding a plug of wood which was attached to a leader rope,
swim to the shore to the waiting fishermen after the net had
been laid. The technique was a good one. By laying the net in
a parallel line to the shore and by sending a dog swimming in
with the leader, it saved much effort on behalf of the boatman.

He was also the principal dog of the market gunners,
although in areas where the Chesapeake Bay retriever was more
popular, he was probably used to a lesser extent. Before the
advent of the deep freeze, or factory farming, large numbers of
coastal inhabitants would commercially shoot wildfowl to service the markets up and down the population centres of the
eastern seaboard, and this was the activity where the dog was
to prove his greatest service. Possessed of enormous stamina,
with bulky shoulders, dense waterproof coats and superb marking ability, they would enter the water repeatedly as they retrieved bird after bird. A hundred retrieves in a day was not
unusual, with some really superior individuals reputed to have
retrieved up to 200 birds in a day. They also had the remarkable
capacity of being able to mark up to six birds down at a time.

Today the labrador is still by far the most popular retriever
of the gundog breeds, not only as a working dog, but also on
the show bench, and this has resulted in there being two distinct and separate categories of labrador. The dogs bred for
the show-bench have their emphasis put on looks alone, and
although there are a few owners who also train their dogs for
the gun, the majority of showdogs are never used for any form
of field sports. At the other end of the scale are the trialing
dogs. Field trialing has developed into a highly competitive
activity with large sums of money to be earned from stud fees
from a champion dog, and as it has become more competitive,
greater emphasis has been put on the dog's speed and mental
capabilities. This has resulted in strains of the trialing dogs

progressively getting further away from the actual standard of the breed, with some highly qualified trialing individuals that have reached Field Trials Champion status bearing little resemblance to the traditional labrador, with their snipey, pointed heads, curly tails and narrow shoulders. Although some of these auspicious dogs may be excellent in the field, they would not survive particularly well if they were to be transported back to compete in work with their forebears. It is however entirely possible to find many dogs in this country that do conform to the physical attributes desirable in the standard, whilst at the same time having impeccable trialing/working blood in their veins.

Three young labrador bitches with eyes only for the handler.

For the man who wants a malleable, easily trained and maintained dog, the labrador is the obvious choice, for he, more than any other dog in the shooting field, is the supreme retriever, whether he is required to battle through icy seas during a coastal fowling trip, or merely to pick a pheasant from a root field. But it is when that pheasant has run off, doing his best to hide and avoid capture, that the labrador's scenting powers prove his supremacy, and few birds can successfully give an experienced labrador the slip. Then again, the potential dog buyer must ask himself what type of shooting he is intending to do. In the main it is due to trialing that the idea has come about that a labrador is not a hunting dog. All dogs are capable of hunting, some merely do it better than others. For the sportsman who puts greater emphasis on retrieving but wants a dog that will quarter in front of him, albeit not as successfully and not with as much flair as either a spaniel or a pointer, then a labrador is an entirely acceptable choice.

Standard of the Breed

General appearance – The general appearance of the labrador should be that of a strongly-built, short-coupled, very active dog, broad in the skull, broad and deep through the chest and ribs, broad and strong over the loins and hindquarters. The coat close, short with dense undercoat and free from feather. The dog must move neither too wide nor too close in front or behind, he must stand and move true all round on legs and feet.

Head and skull – The skull should be broad with a pronounced stop so that the skull is not in a straight line with the nose. The head should be clean-cut without fleshy cheeks. The jaws should be medium length and powerful and free from snipiness. The nose wide and the nostrils well developed.

Eyes – The eyes of medium size expressing intelligence and good temper, should be brown or hazel.

Ears – Should not be large and heavy and should hang close to the head, and set rather far back.

Mouth – Teeth should be sound and strong. The lower teeth just behind but touching the upper.

Neck – Should be clean, strong and powerful, and set into well-placed shoulders.

Forequarters – The shoulders should be long and sloping. The forelegs well boned and straight form the shoulder to the ground when viewed from either the front or side. The dog must move neither too wide nor too close in front.

Body – The chest must be of good width and depth with well-sprung ribs. The back should be short coupled.

Hindquarters – The loins must be wide and strong with well-turned stifles; hindquarters well developed and not sloping to the tail. The hocks should be slightly bent and the dog must neither be cow-hocked nor move too wide or too close behind.

Feet – Should be round and compact with well-arched toes and well-developed pads.

Tail – The tail is a distinctive feature of the breed: it should be very thick towards the base, gradually tapering towards the tip, of medium length and practically free from any feathering, but clothed thickly all round with the labrador's short, thick, dense coat, thus giving that peculiar 'rounded' appearance which has been described as the 'Otter' tail. The tail may be carried gaily, but should not curl over the back.

Coat – The coat is another distinctive feature of the breed: it should be short and dense and without wave, with a weather-resisting undercoat and should give a fairly hard feeling to the hand.

Colour – The colour is generally black or yellow – but other whole colours are permitted. The coat should be free from any white markings but a small white spot on the chest is allowable. The coat should be of a whole colour and not of a flecked appearance.

Weight and size – Desired height for dogs: 56–57cm (22–22½in), bitches 54–56cm (21½–22in).

Faults – Under or overshot mouth; no undercoat; bad action; feathering; snipiness on the head; large or heavy ears; cow-hocked; tail curled over back.

Note – Male animals should have two apparently normal testicles fully descended into the scrotum.

FLATCOATED RETRIEVER

Probably the prettiest, and certainly the most elegant-looking of all the retrievers is the flatcoat, and at one time, during the period around the early 1900s, he was the natural choice for the fashionable shooting man. It is difficult to know quite how much work or planning was put into the development of the breed, but it must have been considerable. Mr SE Shirley of Ettington (1844–1904) who also has the distinction of being the founder of the Kennel Club, originated the modern flatcoat during the 1860s in England, initially from the combination of breeding together labradors and newfoundlands, both specialist

Flatcoated retriever.

water dogs from the north-eastern coast of the American continent. Originally the breed was known as the wavy-coated retriever, but although the dog was reputed to be an excellent worker, his bulky, heavy coat was found to cause him unnecessary effort in the water, restricting the amount of work he could do because much of his energy was spent in propelling himself. As a result, the heavy bulky coat was gradually bred out of the breed until he became known as the flatcoated retriever.

To look at one of these dogs, with their elegant lines, aristocratic carriage and general flair, it is easy to see the influence of both Irish and Gordon setters, and possibly even pointer, who are all credited with being introduced to the breed to acheive their fine looks.

Before the labrador came to real prominence, the flatcoat was regarded as the gentleman's shooting dog, but the labrador, who generally displayed greater speed and agility coupled with superior water work, pushed the flatcoat into second place.

In the working field the flatcoat is truly excellent, and there is little to choose between a good flatcoat and a labrador, so it is difficult to understand why the dog should ever have fallen from popularity. It is probably due to simple taste and fashion change, and as is common in so many field sports matters, the public tend to follow current trends. But he is truly an excellent dog, and the shooting man who likes his looks and wants to be a little different, could certainly buy one of these dogs with confidence, if he can find a dog of proven working ancestry – for sadly the flatcoat falls into the category of being popular as a showdog. This is a testimony to his fine looks and even temperament, but it makes it difficult to find truly working dogs. Another sad fact about this delightful breed is that although some are run in trials, they are largely in amateur hands, so the breed is seldom given an opportunity to really show its worth.

Standard of the Breed

General appearance – A bright, active dog of medium size with an intelligent expression, showing power without lumber, and raciness without weediness.

Head and skull – The head should be long and nicely moulded. The skull flat and moderately broad. There should be a depression or stop between the eyes, slight and in no way accentuated, so as to avoid giving either a down or a dish-faced appearance. The nose of a good size, with open nostrils. The jaws should be long and strong, with a capacity of carrying a hare or pheasant.

Eyes – Should be of medium size, dark-brown or hazel, with a very intelligent expression (a round, prominent eye is a disfigurement) and they should not be obliquely placed.

Ears – Should be small and well set-on, close to the side of the head.

Neck – The head should be well set in the neck, which latter should be long and free from throatiness, symmetrically set and obliquely placed in shoulders running well into the back to allow of easily seeking for the trail.

Forequarters – The chest should be deep and fairly broad, with a well-defined brisket, on which the elbows should work cleanly and evenly. The legs are of the greatest importance, the forelegs should be perfectly straight, with the bone of good quality carried right down to the feet and when the dog is in full coat the legs should be well feathered.

Body – The fore-ribs should be fairly flat, showing a gradual spring and well-arched in the centre of the body, but rather lighter towards the quarters. Open couplings are to be ruthlessly condemned. The back should be short, square and well ribbed up.

Hindquarters – Should be muscular. The stifle should not be too straight or too bent, and the dog must neither be cow-hocked nor move too widely behind, in fact he must stand and move true on legs and feet all round. The legs should be well feathered.

Feet – Should be round and strong with toes close and well arched, the soles being thick and strong.

Gait – Free and flowing, straight and true as seen from front and rear.

Tail – Short, straight and well set on, carried gaily, but never much above the level of the back.

Coat – Should be dense, of fine quality and texture, flat as possible.

Colour – Black or liver.

Weight and size – Should be between 27.2 and 31.8 kg (60–70lb).

Note – Male animals should have two apparently normal testicles fully descended into the scrotum.

GOLDEN RETRIEVER

Although a popular retrieving breed, the golden retriever has largely gone to the show-bench, mainly because of its beautiful golden coat, gentle nature and kind disposition. There are still many goldies used in the shooting field, however.

The breed originated at the kennel of Lord Tweedmouth who had purchased a wavy-coated retriever and which in 1868 he used to service a bitch of local breeding referred to as a Tweed water spaniel. The issue of this union was Primrose, Ada, Cowslip and Crocus. From these four animals the golden retriever of today has its origins. Although generally not fast or powerful with water work, some goldies can be particularly excellent in this environment, though it must be said that since they have a tendency to swim lower in the water, due to their heavy, long coats, they would not be the ideal choice for a wildfowler. If obtained from proven working stock they can be a highly rewarding dog to work with, and the field sportsman who shoots in an environment suitable for this breed can approach the breed with confidence.

The golden retriever generally reaches maturity later than other retrieving breeds. Also, with large numbers of modern shooting men placing a greater emphasis on pride in new cars and not able to enjoy the luxury of being able to kennel a dog, it can be inconvenient to have such a long-haired animal. To keep it looking its best, time must be taken to maintain its coat, which can pick up and retain dirt and burrs more readily than one of its shorter-haired cousins.

Standard of the Breed

General appearance – Should be of a symmetrical, active, powerful dog, a good level mover, sound and well put together, with a kindly expression, not clumsy nor long in the leg.
Head and skull – Broad skull, well set on a clean and muscular neck, muzzle powerful and wide, not weak-jawed, good stop.
Eyes – Dark and set well apart, very kindly in expression, with dark rims.
Ears – Well proportioned, of moderate size, and well set on.
Mouth – Teeth should be sound and strong. Neither overshot nor undershot, the lower teeth just behind but touching the upper.
Neck – The neck should be clean and muscular.
Forequarters – The forelegs should be straight, with good bone. Shoulders should be well laid back and long in the blade.
Body – Well-balanced, short coupled, and deep through the heart. Ribs deep and well sprung.
Hindquarters – The loins and legs should be strong and muscular, with good second thighs and well-bent stifles. Hocks well let down, not cow-hocked.
Feet – Round and cat-like, not open or splay.
Tail – Should not be carried too gaily nor curled at the tip.
Coat – Should be flat or wavy with good feathering, and a dense, water-resisting undercoat.
Colour – Any shade of gold or cream, but neither red nor mahogany. The presence of a few white hairs on chest permissible. White collar, feet, toes or blaze should be penalised. Nose should be black.
Weight and size – The average weight in good hard condition should be: dogs 32–37kg (70–80lb); bitches 27–32kg (60–70lb).

Height at shoulder: dogs 56–61cm (22–24in); bitches 51–56cm (20–22in).
Note – Male animals should have two apparently normal testicles fully descended into the scrotum.

CURLY-COATED RETRIEVER

For the man who is prepared to put a lot of work and devotion into his dog; who is able to keep him with him, preferably in the house, at least for part of the time; who wants a dog with individuality; a dog that is not for the social shooter, standing at a peg, but more for the true wildfowler, then there is no better choice of dog than the curly-coated retriever. This big, tough, strong dog is without doubt the best of the retrievers for the true wildfowler who is able to train and handle this rewarding breed.

Curly-coated retriever.

The largest and most individual of the retrievers, the curly is probably the result of the cross-breeding of the standard poodle, the Irish water spaniel and the labrador, and first appeared in England in the nineteenth century. It is strange that such a potentially fabulous water dog has never become more popular with the many thousands of rough shooters and fowlers. But this is probably in part due to fashion – he is not a demonstrative as a golden retriever, or as elegantly good looking as a flatcoat. He is not as quick as the labrador, neither is he as easily trained. It is in his training that he is probably most demanding, since curlys generally require more knowledgeable handling. A labrador, for instance, is more forgiving if the handler makes mistakes – not so the curly. He is slow to mature, and is not really fully developed into complete adulthood until he is three years old, and, as I have said, he is not an easily trained dog since they are very much individuals. The only way I know of really making a success with a curly is to get to know him really well, to understand the way the dog thinks, to appreciate how he works out a problem, to work together with him, to be the essence of patience, and to combine firmness with sensible gentle handling, and, at the end of the day, the curly will be the sort of gundog you will be proud to shoot with.

The most distinctive feature of this dog is of course the coat, which is made up of tiny tight curls of dense hair, so tightly packed that the coat is not only impenetrable to any form of comb or brush, but provides a perfect protection from the most daunting of cover, which the curly will happily push through if required. The coat is of course the very essence of water repellance. It also traps a thin layer of air when the dog enters water which acts as insulation from the cold. A small bonus with the coat is that the air trapped also gives extra buoyancy to the dog in water. The curly is also, because of his temperament, more a one man dog than any of the other retrievers. He will identify with his home more than other breeds and in consequence is certainly an excellent watchdog.

One seldom sees curlys at shows. They have never caught the public imagination as much as the other more showy, gentle, and sheer good-looking retrievers.

Standard of the Breed

General appearance – A strong smart upstanding dog showing activity, endurance and intelligence.

Head and skull – Long, well-proportioned flat skull, jaws strong and long but not inclined to snipiness. Nose black in the

Curly-coated retriever.

black-coated variety with wide nostrils, coarseness of head to be deprecated.

Eyes – Black or brown but not 'gooseberry' coloured, rather large but not too prominent.

Ears – Rather small, set on low, lying close to the head and covered with short curls.

Mouth – Teeth strong and level.

Neck – Should be moderately long, free from throatiness.

Forequarters – Shoulders should be very deep, muscular and well laid back.

Hindquarters – Strong and muscular, hock low to the ground with good bend to stifle and hock.

Body – Well-sprung ribs, good depth of brisket, not too long in the loin, as little tucked-up in flank as possible.

Feet – Round and compact with well-arched toes.

Gait – Covering plenty of ground with drive.

Tail – Moderately short, carried fairly straight and covered with curls, tapering towards the point, gay tail not desirable.

Coat – Should be one mass of crisp small curls all over. This being the main characteristic of the breed should be given great consideration when making judging awards.

Colour – Black or liver.

Size – Desirable height at withers: dogs 68.58cm (27in); bitches 63.50cm (25in).

Faults – Wide skull, light eyes, curled tail and bad movement.

Note – Male animals should have two apparently normal testicles fully descended into the scrotum.

SPANIELS

ENGLISH SPRINGER SPANIEL

To see a good English springer spaniel (ESS) as he works away merrily, quartering in front of the gun, dropping to flush as he 'springs' game, dashing forward on command to retrieve shot game, and bringing it back to the handler, is a joy, to anyone who is interested in gundogs of any kind, for the springer is indeed a most useful and exciting little dog. But it has been said that whilst you can put up with a half-trained labrador and learn to live with it, a half-trained springer can be an uncontrolled nightmare. This is certainly true of any dog, but the reason it is said with regard to springers is that by the very nature of his type of character and work, he is a busy little dog, whizzing through the cover, and if he is not trained to harness his energy into a controlled work pattern, he can quickly get out of control and end up running wild.

The springer is probably the oldest of the 'land' spaniels. One theory is that they may have been first brought to Britain by the Romans. Remembering that the Romans are credited with the introduction of both the rabbit and the fallow deer, which were brought to Britain as food sources, it is entirely likely that they would have brought their dogs with them. The name 'spaniel' refers to the generally accepted theory that they originated in Spain. It is certain that they were in Britain 600 years ago, since a Dr Cauis, personal physician to Edward VI, and also a dog enthusiast, wrote in his 'History of English Dogges' in the mid-sixteenth century of the springers origins, describing a dog that sprang game for the hunter. It is also certain that the springers of today are the product of many serious breeding experiments over many years. It would be true to say that of all the types of spaniel in use as gundogs, the springer is certainly the most versatile and widely used, and the general image of so many rough shooters and countrymen is one of them with a springer at heel.

English springer spaniel.

The springer is certainly the best of the hunting dogs in Britain, yet has the ability to gently retrieve from both land and water. Although the standard of the breed is reproduced here, it must be said that the springer has very much developed into two distinct strains of dog – working and show – and whilst with other breeds such as the curly-coated and flatcoated retrievers it can be difficult for the potential buyer to find a strain of dog that is entirely work bred (many of them being dual dogs used for both show-bench and work) with the springer this is very much the opposite. The average shooting springer differs considerably from the standard and in show springers much of the working instinct has been lost. So it is imperative that anyone who wishes to buy a springer spaniel puppy to be used for the gun must satisfy himself that the dog is from an impeccable working pedigree.

Standard of the Breed

Characteristics – The English springer is the oldest of our sporting gundogs and the taproot from which all of our sporting land spaniels (Clumbers excepted) have been evolved. It was originally used for the purpose of finding and springing game for the net, falcon, or greyhound, but at the present time it is used entirely to find, flush and retrieve game for the gun. The breed is of ancient and pure origin, and should be kept as such.

General appearance – The general appearance of the modern springer is that of a symmetrical, compact, strong, upstanding, merry, and active dog, built for endurance and activity. He is the highest on the leg and raciest in build of all British land spaniels.

Head and skull – The skull should be of medium length and fairly broad and slightly rounded, rising from the foreface, making a brow or stop, divided by a fluting between the eyes gradually dying away along the forehead towards the occiput bone, which should not be peaked. The cheeks should be flat, that is not rounded or full. The foreface should be of proportionate length to the skull, fairly broad and deep without being coarse, well chiselled below the eyes, fairly deep and square in flew, but not exaggerated to such an extent as would interfere with comfort when retrieving. Nostrils well developed.

Eyes – The eyes should be neither too full nor too small but of medium size, not prominent nor sunken but well set in (not showing haw) of an alert, kind expression. A mouse-like eye without expression is objectionable, as also is a light eye. The colour should be dark hazel.

Ears – The ears should be lobular in shape, set close to the head, of good length and width, but not exaggerated. The correct set should be in line with the eye.

Mouth – The jaws should be strong, with a perfect regular and complete scissor bite, i.e. the upper teeth closely overlapping the lower teeth and set square to the jaws.

Neck – The neck should be strong and muscular, of nice length and free from throatiness, well set in the shoulders, nicely arched and tapering towards the head – thus giving great activity and speed. A ewe neck is objectionable.

Forequarters – The forelegs should be straight and nicely feathered, elbows set well to body and with proportionate substance to carry the body, strong flexible pasterns.

English springer spaniel.

Body – The body should be strong and of proportionate length, neither too long nor too short, the chest deep and well developed with plenty of heart and lung room, well sprung ribs; loin muscular and strong with slight arch, and well coupled; thighs broad and muscular and well developed.

Hindquarters – The hindlegs should be well let down from hip to hocks. Stifles and hocks moderately bent, inclining neither inwards nor outwards. Coarseness of hocks objectionable.

Feet – Feet tight, compact, and well rounded with strong full pads.

Gait The springer's gait is strictly his own. His forelegs should swing straight forward from the shoulder throwing the feet well forward in an easy and free manner. His hocks should drive well under his body, following in a line with the forelegs. At slow movements many springers have a pacing stride typical of the breed.

Tail – The stern should be low and never carried above the level of the back, well feathered and with a lively action.

Coat – The coat should be close, straight, and weather-resisting without being coarse.

Colour – Any recognised land spaniel colour is acceptable, but liver and white, black and white, or either of these colours with tan markings preferred.

Weight and size – The approximate height should be 51cm (20in). The approximate weight should be 22.7kg (50lb).

Note – Male animals should have two apparently normal testicles fully descended into the scrotum.

WELSH SPRINGER SPANIEL

To non-springer spaniel enthusiasts the Welsh and English springers are normally lumped together simply as springers, yet they are in fact two entirely different breeds, with certain differences between them. The Welsh springer is more difficult to train in that he is more intent on hunting away, and a great deal of care and patience must be taken to keep his attention. Smaller than the English springer, his coat is of a dark rich red and white colouration. The Welsh springer is a fabulously energetic little dog, and as far as work is concerned there is little to choose between either the English or the Welsh. Unfortunately however, true working strains are not as easily found in the Welsh springers as their larger English cousins.

Standard of the Breed

Characteristics – The Welsh spaniel or 'springer' is also known and referred to in Wales as a 'starter'. He is of very ancient and pure origin, and is a distinct variety.

General appearance – A symmetrical, compact, strong, merry, very active dog, not stilty; obviously built for endurance and hard work. A quick and active mover displaying plenty of push and drive.

Head and skull – Skull proportionate, of moderate length, slightly domed, with clearly defined stop and well chiselled below the eyes. Muzzle of medium length, straight, fairly square, the nostrils well developed and flesh-coloured or dark. A short chubby head is objectionable.

Eyes – Hazel or dark, medium size, not prominent, nor sunken, nor showing haw.

Ears – Set moderately low and hanging close to the cheeks, comparatively small and gradually narrowing towards the lip and shaped somewhat like a vine leaf, covered with setter-like feathering.

Mouth – The jaws should be strong, with a perfect regular and complete scissor bite, i.e. the upper teeth closely overlapping the lower teeth and set square to the jaws.

Neck – Long and muscular, clean in throat, neatly set into long, sloping shoulders.

Forequarters – Forelegs of medium length, straight, well boned, moderately feathered.

Body – Not long: strong and muscular with deep brisket, well-sprung ribs; length of body should be proportionate to length of leg, and very well balanced; muscular loin slightly arched and well coupled up.

Hindquarters – Strong and muscular, wide and fully developed with deep second thighs. Hind legs well boned, hocks well let down; stifles moderately bent (neither turned in nor out) moderately feathered.

Feet – Round, with thick pads. Firm and cat-like, not too large or spreading.

Tail – Well set on and low, never carried above the level of the back, lightly feathered and lively in action.

Coat – Straight or flat, of a nice silky texture, never wiry nor wavy. A curly coat is most objectionable.

Colour – Rich red and white only.

Weight and size – A dog not to exceed 48cm (19in) in height at shoulder and a bitch 46cm (18in) approximately.

Faults – Any departure from the foregoing points should be considered a fault and the seriousness of the fault should be in exact proportion to its degree.

Note – Male animals should have two apparently normal testicles fully descended into the scrotum.

HUNTING POINTING RETRIEVING BREEDS

GERMAN SHORTHAIRED POINTER

Dog owners have very individual tastes when it comes to a dog's looks. Some people who are 'spaniel' men can see little to admire in an HPR dog, finding them not to their taste. Yet to others, the HPR's are the epitome of grace and beauty.

The German shorthaired pointer (GSP) is undoubtedly the most popular of the HPR dogs in Britain today, and they have, over the last few years, gained an increasing number of enthusiasts who have taken this breed very much to heart, captivated by his sheer versatility in the field and his fabulous good looks. Whilst it is a pleasure to watch any working dog as he carries out the tasks he has been trained for – the springer bustling through cover or the labrador doing a long distance retrieve on a difficult runner – it is the excellence with which some of these dogs carry out the job that appeals and attracts, not necessarily the dog's physical good looks. This is not the case with the HPR dogs, and the GSP in particular, for to the enthusiast of the breed they have the added bonus of being physically pleasing to the eye as they work. With their short coats and well-muscled configuration they display a grace and athleticism in some ways almost feline.

The forerunners of the GSP began in the seventeenth century, with the combination of Spanish pointer and schweisshund. The pointer gave the strain the ability to point game and the schweisshund (a tracking hound not dissimilar to our own bloodhound) introduced the ability to follow scent. This was the basis of the German pointer. A later introduction of the 'English-style' pointer gave the breed a lighter, more stream-lined and generally faster influence, with the additional input of retriever blood and foxhound blood. It is from these origins that the GSP was evolved by the careful and diligent breeding of the best specimens. This has resulted in the dog of today having the best attributes of the specialists – the retrieving ability of the retriever, the persistence on a scent of the blood-hound, the pointing characteristics of the pointer and the keen hunting instincts of the foxhound.

The GSP is ideally suited to the man who shoots, either on his own or in the company of one or two friends. He is not

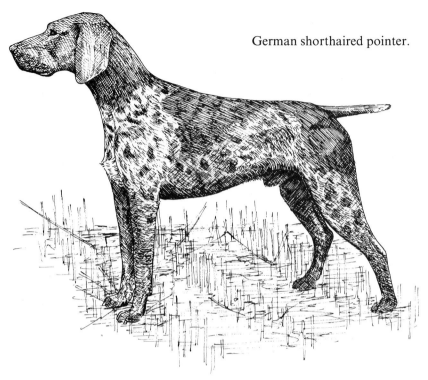

German shorthaired pointer.

suitable for the man who walks game in the company of several others, since he must range widely on either side of the gun and is likely to go on point further down the line. This gives the gun the immediate problem of who shoots the bird; the man who the dog is pointing in front of and who by rights should have the game, or should the handler break line and go to the dog? Neither is the GSP suitable as a peg dog with the formality of steady and controlled retrieving. To use a GSP for any one of his multiple abilities alone would be unwise, and a waste, for the specialist retrievers or spaniels will do these tasks with greater efficiency. Where the GSP comes into his own is when he is used with all his functions coming into play, and for the rough shooter who wants one dog with the abilities of so many, then the GSP is an excellent choice.

Standard of the Breed
Characteristics – The German shorthaired pointer is a dual-purpose pointer-retriever and this accounts for his excellence in the field, which requires a very keen nose, perseverance in searching, and enterprise. His style attracts attention; he is

equally good on land and in water, is biddable, an extremely keen worker, and very loyal.

General appearance – A noble, steady dog showing power, endurance and speed, giving the immediate impression of an alert and energetic (not nervous) dog whose movements are well co-ordinated. Neither unduly small nor conspicuously large, but of medium size, and like the hunter, 'With a short back stands over plenty of ground'. Grace of outline, clean cut head, sloping long shoulders, deep chest, short back and powerful hindquarters, good bone composition, adequate muscle, well carried tail and taut coat giving a thoroughbred appearance.

Head and skull – Clean-cut, neither too light nor too heavy, but well proportioned to the body. The skull sufficiently broad and slightly rounded. The furrow between the eyes not so deep, and the occiput not so pronounced as in the English pointer. The nasal bone rises gradually from nose to forehead (this is more pronounced in the male) and should never possess a definite stop as in the English pointer, but when viewed from the side there is a well-defined stop effect due to the position of the

German shorthaired pointer.

eyebrows. The lips fall away almost vertically from a somewhat protruding nose and continue in a slight curve to the corner of the mouth. Lips well developed but not over hung. Jaws powerful and sufficiently long to enable the dog to pick up and carry game. Dish-faced and snipy muzzle are not desirable. Nose solid brown, wide nostrils well opened and soft.

Eyes – Medium size, soft and intelligent, not protruding nor too deep set. Varying in shades of brown to tone with coat. Light eye not desirable. Eyelids should close properly.

Ears – Broad and set high; neither too fleshy nor too thin with a short soft coat; hung close to the head, no pronounced fold, rounded at the tip and should reach almost to the corner of the mouth when brought forward.

Mouth – Teeth sound and strong. Molar teeth meeting exactly and the eyeteeth should fit close in a true scissor bite. Neither overshot nor undershot.

Neck – Moderately long, muscular and slightly arched, becoming larger towards the shoulders. Skin should not fit too closely.

Forequarters – Shoulder sloping and very muscular with top of shoulder-blades close; upper arm bones between shoulder and elbow long. Elbows well laid back, neither pointing outwards nor inwards. Forelegs straight and lean, sufficiently muscular and strong but not coarse-boned. Pasterns slightly sloping, almost straight but not quite.

Body – Chest must appear deep rather than wide but not out of proportion to the rest of the body; ribs deep and well sprung, never barrel-shaped nor flat as in the hound; back ribs reaching well down to tucked up loins. Chest measurement immediately behind the elbows smaller than about a hand's-breadth behind the elbows, so that the upper arm has freedom of movement. Firm, short back, not arched. The loin wide and slightly arched, the croup wide and sufficiently long, neither too heavy nor too sloping, starting on a level with the back and sloping gradually towards the tail. Bones solid and strong not clumsy and porous.

Hindquarters – The hips broad and wide falling slightly towards the tail. Thighs strong and well muscled. Stifles well bent. Hocks square with the body and slightly bent, turning neither in nor out. Pasterns nearly upright.

Feet – Compact, close-knit, round to spoon-shaped, well padded, should turn neither in nor out. Toes well arched and heavy nailed.

Tail – Starts high and thick growing gradually thinner. Docked to medium length by two-fifths to half its length. When quiet, tail should be carried down, and when moving, horizontally, never held high over the back or bent.

Coat – Skin should not fit loosely or fold. Coat short, flat and coarse to the touch, slightly longer under the tail.

Colour – Solid liver, liver and white spotted, liver and white spotted and ticked, liver and white ticked, black and white.

Weight and size – Dogs 25–31.8kg (55–70lb); bitches 24.4–27.2kg (45–60lb). Size – dogs 58–64cm (23–25in) and bitches 53–59cm (21–23in) at the shoulder. Symmetry is most essential.

Faults – Bone structure too clumsy, sway-back, head too large, deep wrinkles in forehead, cone-shaped skull or occiput too prominent. Ears too long or too closely set together, eyelids not closing properly. Wrinkles in neck. Feet or elbows turned inwards or outwards. Soft, sunken, or splayed toes; cowhocks, straight hindlegs, or down on pasterns. Tail starting too low, undocked, too thick, curled up or too furry. Tri-coloured.

Note – Male animals should have two apparently normal testicles fully descended into the scrotum.

German pointer puppy investigates a toad.

LARGE MUNSTERLANDER

The first Large Munsterlander was imported into Britain as recently as 1971, yet this interesting dog cannot be ignored in any discussion on pointer retrievers. Although a recent addition to the British gundog scene, the munsterlander has of course been well used in Germany for as long as most of their other gundog breeds. In fact, it is dogs very similar to the munsterlander that appear so often in many old paintings depicting hunting scenes in Germany, although they are often either brown and white, black and white or tri-coloured.

Before the nineteenth century, hunting dogs were judged purely by their ability, and it made good sense to put together the best dogs and bitches, irrespective of colouration, but in the early nineteenth century hunting dog owners and enthusiasts became more conscious of both colour and physical standards, establishing records which recorded which dogs had been bred with each other and the results of the mating. In the case of the Large Munsterlander fashion dictated that the darker colours were more desirable, and that the lighter coloured pups should be culled at birth. The breed at that time was regarded as a longhaired German pointer. With the foundation of the German Kennel Club and the establishment of a general studbook, only brown and white longhaired German pointers were permitted to be registered. Any black and white dogs were disallowed, and since they had little value they were discarded, being destroyed or passed on to the grateful hands of the local jägers, foresters and farmers. These individuals had less concern for fashion or officialdom, and no doubt rejoiced at this source of quality dogs, rejected for the seemingly trivial reason of colour alone. So there survived in the Munster region of Germany a whole population of black and white working dogs. It is of course from this area that the breed takes its name.

It was not until 1919, with the formation of a club to try to officially bring all the specimens together and establish a distinct breed, that the munsterlander was officially recognised and given the name of black and white Large Munsterlander. I have seen munsterlanders working in a variety of cover conditions and terrain, and they well deserve their reputation as being excellent and worthwhile dogs.

Interim Standard
Characteristics – The Large Munsterlander is a multi-purpose gundog, ideal for the rough shooter. He has an excellent nose, staying power, and works equally well on land and in water. A

keen worker, easily taught, loyal, affectionate and trustworthy.

General appearance – Alert and energetic, with a strong muscular body, having good movement with drive.

Head and skull – Well proportioned to the body, elongated. Skull sufficiently broad, slightly rounded, with no pronounced occiput. Strong jaw muscles, well formed black nose, wide soft nostril, slight rise from the nasal bone to the forehead but no pronounced stop. Lips slightly rounded, and well fitting.

Eyes – Intelligent, medium size, dark brown, not deep set or protruding. No haw showing.

Ears – Broad and set high, lying flat and close to the head, with a rounded tip. Hair on the ears should be long, extending beyond the tip.

Mouth – Strong and sound, with well-developed teeth, faultless scissor bite and molars meeting exactly.

Neck – Strong, muscular, slightly arched, joining the shoulder and chest smoothly.

Forequarters – Chest wide and with good depth of brisket. Shoulders well laid back, forelegs straight, pasterns strong.

Body – Firm strong back, short coupled, slightly higher at the shoulder, sloping smoothly towards the croup and tail. Wide well-muscled loin. Wide croup. Ribs well sprung, deep and reaching well up to the loins. Taut abdomen, slightly tucked up.

Hindquarters – Hips broad. Well-muscled thighs, well-turned stifles, hocks well let down. Hind dew claws must be removed on stock born after January 1982.

Feet – Tight, moderately rounded and well-knuckled with dense hair between the toes. Strong nails.

Gait – Free, long striding springy gait.

Tail – Well set on, in line with the back. Base thick, tapering evenly towards the tip, well feathered. It should be carried horizontally or curved slightly upwards. Docking optional, to the first or second joint from the tip.

Coat – Hair long and dense, but not curly or coarse. Well feathered on front and hind legs and on tail, more so in dogs than in bitches. The hair must lie short and smooth on the head.

Colour – Head solid black, white blaze, snip or star allowed. Body white with black patches, flecked, ticked or combination of these.

Size – Dogs 60–65cm (23½–25½in); bitches 58–63cm (22¼–24¾in).
Faults – Any departure from the foregoing points should be considered a fault and the seriousness of the fault should be in exact proportion to its degree.
Note – Male animals should have two apparently normal testicles fully descended into the scrotum.

HUNGARIAN VIZSLA

Although the vizsla is thought of as a Hungarian dog, it has its origins further to the east. The word 'vizsla' is Turkish, meaning 'sleek'. They are also sometimes referred to as the Magyar, which bears reference to the invading eastern warriors. One must remember that much of Europe was settled originally from the east, and many dogs were brought with these eastern invaders. The Turks who occupied Hungary for a large part of the sixteenth and seventeenth centuries are credited with having introduced the pointer-type dog, which was yellow in colour, and it is likely that it was crossed with the local hound, the copo, to form the main ancestry of the vizsla.

It was during the period of the Austro-Hungarian Empire, when the nobility, like the nobilities of other European countries, concentrated greatly on the sport of hunting and vast tracts of land were made over to sport. With game of all types available, including boars, wolves, deer, ground game and wildfowl, these dogs really came into prominence, being bred in kennels owned by the nobility. The dog is basically the Hungarian equivalent of the GSP, with slightly different attributes to accommodate the terrain of his origins.

The vizsla falls into the category of being an excellent HPR dog and is generally steadier and quieter than the weimaraner although very similar. They are not common and it is difficult to find one from impeccable working stock.

Standard of the Breed
Characteristics – The Hungarian vizsla should be lively and intelligent, obedient but sensitive, very affectionate and easily trained. It was bred for hunting for fur and feather on open ground or in thick cover, pointing and retrieving from both land and water.

General appearance – A medium-sized dog of distinguished appearance, robust and not too heavily boned.

Head and skull – The head should be gaunt and noble. The skull should be moderately wide between the ears with a median line down the forehead and a moderate stop. The muzzle should be a little longer than the skull and although tapering should be well squared at the end. The nostrils should be well developed, broad and wide. The jaws strong and powerful. The lips should cover the jaws completely and should be neither loose nor pendulous. The nose should be brown.

Eyes – Neither deep nor prominent, of medium size, being a shade darker in colour than the coat. The shape of the eyes should be slightly oval and the eyelids should fit tightly. A yellow or black eye is objectionable.

Ears – The ears should be moderately low set, proportionately long with a thin skin and hang down close to the cheeks; should be rounded V-shaped not fleshy.

Mouth – Sound white teeth meeting in a scissor bite, full dentition is desirable.

Forequarters – Shoulders should be well laid and muscular, elbow straight pointing neither in nor out, the forearm should be long.

Body – Back should be level, short, well muscled, withers high. The chest should be moderately broad and deep with prominent breast bone. The distance from the withers to the lowest part of the chest should be equal to the distance from the chest to the ground. The ribs should be well sprung and the belly should be tight with a light tuck-up beneath the loin. The croup should be well muscled.

Hindquarters – Should be straight when viewed from the rear, the thighs should be well developed with moderate angulation, the hocks well let down.

Feet – Rounded with toes short, arched and well closed. A cat like foot is desirable, hare foot is objectionable. Nails short, strong, and a shade darker in colour than coat. Dew claws should be removed.

Gait – Graceful and elegant with a lively trot and ground covering gallop.

Tail – Should be of moderate thickness, rather low set, with one third docked off. Whilst moving should be held horizontally.

Coat – Should be short and straight, dense and coarse, and feel greasy to the touch.

Colour – Russet gold. Small white marks on chest and feet, though acceptable, are not desirable.

Weight and size – Optimum weight 22–30kg (48½–66lb). Height at withers: dogs 57–64cm (22½–25in); bitches 53–60cm (21–23½in).

Faults – Any departure from the foregoing points should be considered a fault and the seriousness of the fault should be in exact proportion to its degree.

Note – Male animals should have two apparently normal testicles fully descended into the scrotum.

WEIMARANER

Probably the most distinctive and immediately noticeable point about the weimaraner is his unusual colour, which ranges from a delicate silvery grey to a dark browny grey. So distinctive is his coat that he has been christened the 'Grey' or 'silver ghost' in different parts of America.

With his origins firmly fixed in the noble houses of Germany the dog has a long and distinguished history in that country. The various breeds he has evolved from are difficult to pin down with any certainty, but there have been several theories put forward. In the seventeenth century German hunting paintings, dogs often appear with the same shorthaired coloration and may reflect a purity unbroken since then. It is also theorized that the breed has evolved from cross breeding hounds and pointers, like the GSP, from which he differs not only in size, being larger, but also in his hunting instincts. He has a tendency to be more hound-like, holding his head lower, and using a combination of air and ground scent to find his quarry.

The weimaraner tends to be more aggressive than the GSP, with a very strong guarding instinct for both his home and family, and is more a dog for the enthusiast of the breed, rather than one of the mainstream HPR owners who would probably be better advised to gravitate towards a GSP.

Standard of the Breed

Characteristics – In the case of the weimaraner his hunting ability is the paramount concern and any fault of body or mind which detracts from this ability should be penalised. The dog should display a temperament that is fearless, friendly, protective and obedient.

General appearance – A medium-sized grey dog with light eyes, he should present a picture of great driving power, stamina, alertness and balance. Above all, the dog should indicate ability to work hard in the field. Movement should be effortless and ground covering and should indicate smooth co-ordination. When seen from the rear, the hind feet should parallel the front feet. When seen from the side, the top line should remain strong and level.

Head and skull – Moderately long and aristocratic, with moderate stop and slight median line extending back over the forehead. Rather prominent occipital bone and ears set well back. Measurement from the top of the nose to stop to equal that from the stop to the occipital prominence. The flews should be moderately deep, enclosing a powerful jaw. Foreface perfectly straight, delicate at the nostrils. Skin tightly drawn. Neck clean cut and moderately long. Expression keen, kind and intelligent.

Eyes – Medium sized in shades of amber or blue-grey, not protruding or too deeply set, placed far enough apart to indicate good disposition and intelligence. When dilated under excitement, the eyes may appear almost black.

Ears – Long and lobular, slightly folded and set high. The ear when drawn alongside the jaw should end approximately one inch from the point of the nose.

Mouth – Well set, strong and even teeth, well developed and proportionate to jaw, with correct scissor bite (the upper teeth protruding slightly over the lower teeth). Complete dentition is greatly desired. Grey nose, lips and gums of pinkish flesh shade.

Forequarters – Forelegs straight and strong, with measurement from elbow to the ground equalling the distance from the elbow to the top of the withers.

Body – The length of the body from the highest point of the withers to the root of the tail should equal the measurement from the highest point of the withers to the ground. The top line should be level with a slightly sloping croup. The chest should be well developed and deep, shoulders well laid and snug. Ribs well sprung and long. Abdomen firmly held, moderately tucked up flank. The brisket should drop to the elbow.

Hindquarters – Moderately angulated with well-turned stifle. The hock joint well let down and turned neither in nor out. Musculation well developed.

Feet – Firm and compact. Toes well arched, pads closed and thick. Nails short and grey or amber. Dew claws allowable only on imported dogs.

Tail – Docked at a point such that the tail remaining shall just cover the scrotum in dogs and the vulva in bitches. The thickness of the tail should be in proportion to the body and it should be carried in a manner expressing confidence and sound temperament. In the longhaired weimaraner the tip of the tail should be removed.

Coat – Short, smooth and sleek. In the longhaired weimaraner the coat should be from 1–2 inches long on the body and somewhat longer on the neck, chest and belly. The tail and the back of the limbs should be feathered.

Colour – Preferably silver grey, shades of mouse or roe grey are admissible. The colour usually blends to a lighter shade on head and ears. A dark eel stripe frequently occurs along the back. The whole coat gives an appearance of metallic sheen. Small white mark allowable on chest but not on any other part of the body. White spots that have resulted from injuries should not be penalised. Colour of the longhaired weimaraner as the shorthaired.

Size – Height at withers: dogs 61–69cm (24–27in); bitches 56–64cm (22–25in).

Faults – Shyness or viciousness. Any colour or marking other than specified in this standard.

Note – Male animals should have two apparently normal testicles fully descended into the scrotum.

GERMAN WIREHAIRED POINTER

The German wirehaired pointer is now the most popular shooting dog in Germany and is a breed derived from the shorthaired pointer. But the inclusion of coarser-haired breeds has produced the thick, hard, wiry coat which gives the dog greater protection in cover and keeps him warmer in cold water than his shorterhaired close relation. The GWP is becoming increasingly popular in Britain, but numerically it is far behind the much more popular GSP. Their care and training are identical.

Interim Standard

Characteristics – Wirehaired dual-purpose pointer-retriever excellent in the field with a very keen nose. Perseverance in searching and initiative are required. His style attracts attention; he is equally good on land and in water, is biddable, an extremely keen worker and very loyal.

General appearance – A medium-sized hunting dog of noble bearing, colour unimportant; very harsh hair completely covering the skin, active temperament, intelligent expression, devoted and energetic.

Head and skull – The head should be of medium length with a long strong muzzle.

Eyes – Dark hazel. Bright and intelligent with eyelids closing properly.

Ears – Medium sized.

Mouth – Teeth strong. The jaws should be strong, with a perfect regular and complete scissor bite, i.e. the upper teeth closely overlapping the lower teeth and set square to the jaws.

Neck – Strong and of medium length.

Forequarters – Shoulders sloping and very muscular with top of shoulder-blades close; upper arm bones between shoulder and elbow long. Elbows close to the body, neither pointing outwards nor inwards. Forelegs straight and lean, sufficiently muscular and strong but not coarse-boned. Pasterns slightly sloping, almost straight but not quite.

Body – Chest must appear deep rather than wide but not out of proportion to the rest of the body; ribs deep and well sprung, never barrel-shaped nor flat as in the hound; back ribs reaching well down to tucked up loins. Chest measurement immediately behind the elbows smaller than about a hand's-breadth behind the elbows, so that the upper arm has freedom of movement. Firm, short back, not arched. The loin wide and slightly arched; the croup wide and sufficiently long, neither too heavy nor too sloping starting on a level with the back and sloping gradually towards the tail. Bone solid and strong.

Hindquarters – The hips broad and wide falling slightly towards the tail. Thighs strong and well muscled. Stifles well bent; hocks square with the body and slightly bent, turning neither in nor out. Pasterns nearly upright.

Feet – Compact, close-knit, round to spoon-shaped, well padded, should turn neither in nor out. Toe well arched and heavily nailed.

Gait – Smooth, covering plenty of ground with each stride, driving hind action, elbows neither turning in nor out. Definitely not a hackney action.

Tail – Starts high and thick growing gradually thinner. Docked by half its length. When quiet, tail should be carried down; when moving, horizontally, never held high over the back or bent.

Coat – Hair very harsh, medium length, abundant with a close fitting undercoat. It should not hide the body shape but it should be long enough to give good protection. The coat should lie close to the body. The hair on the lower parts of the legs should be shorter. Very thick on the ears. Bushy eyebrows, full but not over-long beard. Skin fairly fine and close fitting.

Colour – Solid liver, liver and white spotted, liver and white spotted and ticked, liver and white ticked, black and white.

Weight and size – Ideal height at shoulder: 60–65cm ($23\frac{1}{2}$–$25\frac{1}{2}$in); bitches not smaller than 56cm (22in). Weight: dogs 25–32kg (55–$70\frac{1}{2}$lb); bitches $20\frac{1}{2}$–27kg (45–$59\frac{1}{2}$lb).

Faults – Any departure from the foregoing points should be considered a fault and the seriousness with which the fault is regarded should be in exact proportion to its degree.

Note – Male animals should have two apparently normal testicles fully descended into the scrotum.

2. CHOOSING YOUR PUPPY

Once you have decided which particular breed is going to be best suited to your type of sport, also take into account your domestic situation – can the dog be kennelled, do you live in a city flat, are you out at work all day or can someone be at home with the puppy? These factors will, of course, govern both the size of the breed you choose and the age it is best to have the puppy. If you live in a city flat there is little point in having a great bounding GSP or curly-coat when a smaller breed would be less obtrusive and fit in better to your environment. If someone is going to be with the dog all day, then you could consider a small puppy since it is easier to house-train a puppy if he can be watched at all times.

Having made your decision you must remember one important thing which is applicable to all aspects of gundog training from the time of choosing the puppy right through to the end of his training. *You are not in a race.* If you buy or train in haste then you will have years of leisure to regret your urgency. When buying a puppy be prepared to cast your net as wide as possible. The columns of the shooting press normally have plenty of advertisements for quality puppies of all recognised breeds, and while it is more convenient to have to travel only a few miles to buy your puppy, be prepared to travel whatever distance is necessary for the right animal.

Normally advertisements will read that the puppy has been sired by a Field Trial Champion, and the dam is either a good working bitch or is out of a champion dog. Do not consider buying a dog from any other than proven working stock. Whilst there are many good dogs that never see a trial, and can be wonderful workers, the only true indication that the animals are from an exceptional working standard, unless you personally know the owner of both the dog and bitch, is the distinction of the parentage denoted by the field trials awards.

It is best to choose a puppy in the spring since it gives you the summer months, when the weather is kinder, to let the pup grow out of babyhood, avoiding cold and rain when it is unpleasant for you and the pup to be out regularly. There is also the additional problem of the puppy being more susceptible to winter chills and using up vital body-building protein just keeping itself warm.

The first question I am often asked is which sex to have and what are the advantages and disadvantages of male and female dogs. This can be answered fairly simply. There is no difference whatever in their ability to work, although dogs are generally stronger and may have a tendency to be stronger willed. However, dogs do not come into season, with the inconveniences that this brings. A dog, if made up to a champion, can be used for stud, though that is a very small and unlikely consideration for the average shooter. Basically, a dog is just a larger, stronger version of the bitch, able to work twelve months of the year in company. Bitches of course come into season, and during this period they are super-attractive to any dog, which eliminates any chance of you shooting in the company of others who may own dogs. On the other hand, you can take puppies from a bitch in later years, and if you have any intentions of ever doing so, then the choice is made. Bitches have a tendency to be mellower in temperament and generally more prepared to content themselves in a domestic situation. And then there is the last consideration when making a choice of sex quite simply, personal preference. Some dog owners have a marked preference for one sex or the other but when it comes down to pure training and workability, there is no difference.

When you arrive at a kennel to buy a puppy, before you bother to look at the pups and perhaps be swayed by several appealing round and cuddly little bodies, ask if it is possible to see the sire. If a stud dog has been used, then obviously this is normally impossible, but the next question you should ask is to see the pedigree of the puppies where you should find the letters FTCh against several dogs' names.

The pedigree of the litter is extremely important to the potential gundog owner, and a short explanation of the various facets of this often confusing certificate is appropriate. As I have said, unless you know the parents of the puppies personally, the only certain indication that they will be of any use as working dogs are the number of Field Trials Champions, and to a lesser extent, Field Trials Winners to be found in the pedigree.

Although the pedigree normally goes back several generations in the dogs' ancestry, the most important generations are the first three from the left – parent, grand-parents and great-grandparents. If there are Field Trials dogs in any of these generations, hopefully, though not necessarily, on both sides of the pedigree, you can be reasonably certain that your new dog can become an excellent gundog. Both the sire and the dam's line should have proven working dogs in evidence at some point. When looking for Field Trials dogs in the pedigree be careful of two things. The letters FTW can sometimes, quite incorrectly, be used to denote a Field Test Winner. If the breeder is reputable that should not be a problem, but if in doubt do ask. The other title to look out for is the simple CH. This means that the dog is a champion, but this has nothing to do with working ability and denotes a Show Champion, (more frequently shown as ShCh). Once again, if in doubt, ask the breeder.

I have often heard it said that a dog with any show blood in its ancestry should be rejected without question. I do not subscribe to that policy for two reasons. Firstly, I prefer my dogs to be physically attractive and to look as the breed should. Secondly, as long as the show blood is three or more generations removed from the puppy I cannot see how it could adversely affect the working ability of the dog. Indeed it is likely that the show blood was purposefully added to the line to improve the physical appearance of the progeny.

Once you have satisfied yourself that the pedigree is in order, ask to see the puppies. Carefully observe the conditions in which the puppies are kept. If you are taken into the garden shed, and there in the corner is a puppy box covered with excrement and urine, giving you a general feel of poor standards, then this could also give you an indication of what sort of person the breeder is. If on the other hand the puppies are kept in clean, warm surroundings, with only fresh excrement visible (a litter of growing puppies can produce a large amount of excrement in a few hours) then normally the owner of the bitch has higher standards.

Looking at puppies, irrespective of how wonderful they seem, has little bearing on the eventual size and physical appearance

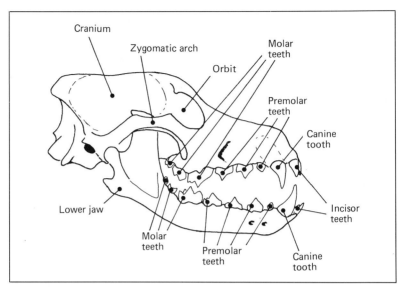

Skull of a dog.

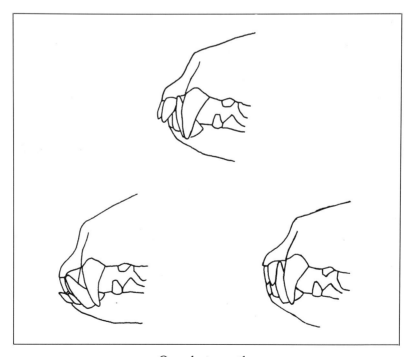

Overshot mouth.

Undershot mouth.   Correct scissor bite.

of the adult dog. Labrador puppies for instance, with their round ball heads, short coupled bodies and little short, thick, otter tails, can in a few months of growth have changed their shape entirely. The round ball head can stretch out into a snipe-like and undesirable line, the little tail can miraculously grow and curl. So the only true guide you will have as to the dogs' adult appearances, is from the parents.

When you are looking at a young puppy open its mouth and check that it has a correct scissor bite, making sure that when its mouth is closed, the teeth of the lower jaw fit neatly behind the teeth of the upper jaw. If there is an undue space between the teeth, the dog would be overshot (see diagram). If, on the other hand, the teeth of the lower jaw protrude beyond the teeth of the upper jaw, the dog would be referred to as undershot (see diagram). Either of these faults must be avoided.

Look at the dog's eyes. Are they the dark standard that the breed requires, or are they light in colour? A light coloured eye should also be avoided. A puppy's legs should be thick, strong and straight. Feet splayed out, bow legs, or any distortion should be left alone. If you are buying a breed which should have the tail docked, look at the length of tail that has been left. A gundog's tail should not be too short, and should look in proportion.

With all puppies the criterion should be that if it is bright and alert and a smaller, plumper version of its parents, with good strong limb bones, then it is a well set up little puppy. If you just cannot make up your mind, and find yourself in doubt, then it is as well to take someone with you who is experienced with puppies.

There are many silly ideas as to the correct way of choosing a puppy, such as sending your child to get it, or stick your hand in to the litter box with eyes closed, and take the first pup you feel. These strange notions stem from the fact that, as I have already said, all puppies change shape and character as they grow up. However, since owning a gundog is a highly personal thing, it is infinitely preferable that you choose an animal that you like right from the outset – one that appeals to you. The best way of doing this is to watch the puppy. Stick your hand in and see which ones are least afraid of you. Is there one that comes in curiosity towards your hand? Is there one that hides in the corner, appearing timid and afraid? Is there a big bold puppy that stands out cheekily from the rest? That is the one to choose. Avoid the timid beast that is afraid of human contact, and go for the one that most appeals. Make sure you get a copy of the pedigree, and put the puppy into your car. It is wise to have taken with you a good stout cardboard box, liberally carpeted with newspapers, since the pup will almost certainly either soil the box on the journey home, or vomit, or both. When you get your puppy home, give him time to settle down in his new surroundings. Try to keep the family back

The correct way of holding a tiny puppy.

from him until he himself comes out looking to see what is going on. Very often this is an anti-climax. You arrive home, having told the family not to crowd around and frighten the pup, and with expectation they watch you carry in the box with the new arrival, supposedly timidly cowering inside. You put it on the floor, and this tiny bundle of fun leaps from the box and proceeds to waddle around the floor, curiously investigating everything, giving no sign of his recent journey, sickness etc.! Still, it is wise to assume that the new arrival will be somewhat timid and strange. It is unlikely that he will ever have seen more than the occasional human face for short periods of time, and will have, up until now, not been away from the comfort of his brothers and sisters, and of course his mother. All of a sudden his whole world changes – bright lights, different smells, and possibly several shrill children, all clamouring to look, touch and hug this wonderful new member of the family. Better therefore to err on the cautious side, and let him investigate both you and your family in his own time.

After he has settled down, it is best to give him a warm meal and bed him down for the night. You will of course have prepared for the new arrival, either by having prepared the kennel where he is to live, or if he is to be kept in the house, a bed in a box, on an uncarpeted floor where any overnight soiling can be easily cleaned.

For the first few nights when a young puppy is away from the nest for the first time, he is likely to yodel and yap, howling for attention. You must understand that this howling is a temporary thing and has to be endured. He will soon realise that if his howling is to no avail and does not result in you coming to see him, it is a pointless exercise, and the howling will stop. There are however a number of things that you can do to help give him comfort, and make the howling less persistent.

Firstly, and most important, any baby or young creature sleeps better on a full stomach. So if you give a puppy a good meal not more than an hour before you want him to bed down for the night, he will not only have moved his bowels quickly after being fed, but be prepared for bed. The sensations that have been taken away from him are a heat source from his brothers and sisters, and of course his mother, the noise of breathing, and, if he is snuggled tight against his mother, her heartbeat. You can do something to simulate these sensations and give him comfort as you wean him away. This is particularly advisable with a young puppy that is a determined and loud howler, particularly if you have neighbours.

An old-fashioned alarm clock, put out of his reach, will give a ticking sound. If you don't possess such a clock, then a quietly playing radio will do. For the heat source the best thing you can do is get one of the old-fashioned stone hot-water bottles.

Pad it well by pushing it inside a couple of thick socks or wrap it well in an old towel and tie it up. The idea is to give him a chew-proof heat source, simulating the warmth and comfort of his mother. A standard hot-water bottle will not do, as he may well burst it. If you cannot procure a stone bottle into which he can cuddle, then try to keep him in a warm environment. This is only a temporary situation, but if you can provide warmth, and a little background noise it will give him comfort, and you more chance of an undisturbed night's sleep.

A young puppy not only represents the beginnings of what is going to be your dreams of your perfect gundog of the future, he also represents an appealing plaything. It is therefore important that you dog train your family by explaining to them that the dog will gain nothing by being endlessly poked, prodded, cuddled, and fed sweets. It is also potentially dangerous for puppies to be lifted by inexperienced hands, as this can put tremendous strain on its internal organs and if dropped, its young soft bones and muscles can be damaged by the fall.

The correct way to lift a puppy is to completely support its stomach. Normally this is best done by passing your arm between its hind legs, with your fingers splayed on its chest. This means the dog is fully supported the entire length of its body, with only its four legs dangling on either side of your arm. The other correct method of lifting a puppy is with one hand supporting its stomach, and the other supporting its chest.

Of course all puppies and young dogs, particularly those being kept indoors, benefit from human contact and playing with children, but this must be kept to a happy medium. Another danger area with a small, appealing puppy is to allow it up on chairs beside you. This is humanising. How is the puppy to know why, as it gets older and larger and having got into the habit as a baby of being allowed on the furniture, you miraculously change the rules, and that this is now disallowed? If you have small children, it is well to remember that puppies can house parasites, and small fingers can transfer a variety of nasty bacteria into small mouths.

Being a family dog as well as a gundog is perfectly acceptable, but it does not mean that your new dog must enjoy the same standards and facilities as one of the family. It is after all a dog, and if kept in its place from puppyhood, many of the problems of later years can be avoided.

3. THE NEW PUPPY

One of the first decisions you will make about your new puppy after you have got it home is its name. I often think that the name of the dog indicates something about the owner. One often meets stoic, unimaginative individuals and inevitably their dogs turn out to have plain, unimaginative, common names. Then again one meets the individual with a bit of imagination, whose dog will have been given a name that has been well thought out. Naming a dog is quite an important act, and must be thought through. There is no point in calling a dog a silly name like Elizabeth or Cleopatra. Rather the name should be short, monosyllabic and easily said. But one does not need to restrict oneself to an endless chain of Bills, Bens, or Sams. A good idea is to look at a map. This often gives inspiration, or think of trees and other country vegetation – Ash, Birch, Bracken, Rowan. But whatever name you call your dog it should be short, and roll off the tongue easily.

HOUSE-TRAINING

Whether your dog is going to be kept in a kennel or as a house dog, it is a good idea to house-train it, and this is easily done if you are prepared to put your mind to it. There is little point in leaving a puppy for long periods of time on its own, then throwing your hands in the air in horror when you come in to discover a puddle on the carpet. Once you become dog conscious it is a relatively simple matter, particularly if you can enlist the help of others in the house. A young dog, when it gets to the point of feeling the need to urinate or defecate, does not understand that this is disallowed in certain areas (i.e. the house). It is the most natural thing for him to do it when the feeling arises. Also because they are like any other baby, they tend to do both functions much more often than adults, partly because their stomachs constantly need something in them, and also because their muscles have not yet developed enough to allow their bodies to hold on to its waste for any length of time. With very small puppies (eight weeks old) it is best just to take them out regularly, always to the same spot, since the smell of their previous visit will encourage the function, and give a bit of praise. Whilst in the house keep an eye on the pup and if he makes any sign that he needs to perform, pick him up and hurry out of doors, giving praise when he performs. Then progressively as the dog is with you over the next few weeks, when it makes the slightest sign go toward it, saying 'no'. Take it by the scruff of the neck and drag it out doors, whereupon as it performs, give praise.

It is inadvisable to frighten the puppy at this stage, and most puppies quickly learn that it is better to go to the door and give some sign of wanting to go out, rather than have the discomfiture of being dragged outside. The word 'no' of course is a very valuable one in dog training, and your dog will, over the coming months of his training period, get to recognise the word as being all-encompassing, indicating your displeasure at any number of acts. If you get up in the morning to be met by the sight of a warm pile of excrement on the floor, there is little point in grabbing the dog, ramming its nose into it, and scolding it. It should suffice to firmly take the dog, show it the crime and say sternly, 'no, no, no', and immediately take the dog out. Most dogs quickly learn what is required of them with house-training, and apart from an occasional accident, the problem disappears.

Regarding the occasional accident, thought must be applied by the owner as to why a house-trained dog will suddenly and inexplicably soil the floor when it is not in the habit of doing so. This applies to dogs of any age. It is normally an indication that either the dog has been left too long and has quite literally been forced to dirty the floor, or may indicate an upset – a chill or sickness – so consider the problem carefully whenever an accident occurs.

Tempting though it often can be just to open your door and let your young pup out on its own to perform its toilet, do not give in to such temptations. A dog that is allowed to go out on its own will get used to being out without you and to having a rake about at whatever goodies it can find. Forgetting for a moment the safety aspects of allowing your dog out on its own, you are in danger of setting a pattern in your young pup's mind – of being able to do as he pleases on his own and therefore out of your control. This does not augur well for his future as a gundog, when he will be asked to remain on his own, but still be under your control.

I am fortunate enough to live in the country, but even here I do not allow my dogs to defecate haphazardly as soon as they are let out of the house or their kennel. It is just as easy to make a pup move away from the house or garden, pavement or play area, as it is to stop it in the house. A stern 'no, no, no' on the first few occasions the pup bends over on your front doorstep, and then running with it to the preferred spot will soon give it the right idea. Please also remember that although it has always been extremely bad mannered and anti-social to allow a dog to defecate on the pavement, it is now illegal, so if your dog shows signs of wishing to do so when you are walking along a pavement, pull it smartly into the gutter.

It does occasionally happen that some dogs that are perfect at any other time will persist in soiling the floor at night. If this is the case, then the best course of action is to alter the dog's feeding habits, giving it less fluid in the latter part of the day, and making the effort to take the animal out for that bit longer before retiring for the night. Another trick to employ if you have a persistent night-time soiler is to quite literally imprison it in its bed. There are few dogs that will actually soil or wet their own beds, and if forcibly kept in a small area will be less inclined to do so.

PARASITES AND CANINE PESTS

A young puppy can act as host to several alarming parasites and is of course susceptible to a variety of canine ailments, some of which can prove fatal. So an understanding of what to look for, and what you are going to guard against, is valuable. It is wise to assume that your young dog is in fact carrying all parasites, and when you take him to the vet for his inoculations, ask him to check the dog's skin for lice or mites. Most vets do this as a matter of course when a young pup is brought in for the first time.

Through their mother's milk puppies are protected for ten to twelve weeks against most diseases. However, this greatly depends on the condition of the bitch and maternal protection must not be assumed to be 100% reliable. Furthermore, in different areas of the country, where diseases are more prevalent, some vets will advise an interim injection fairly early in your pup's life, with the rest of the injections a few weeks later. In other parts of the country which are disease-free, the vet may advise you to wait until twelve weeks for the first injection. The only sensible advice for you to take is that when you buy a puppy and bring it home, inform your vet immediately that you have a puppy, and ask him for his advice as to the timing of the necessary inoculations.

A good example of this is in the area where I live. The local vet would normally advise the first visit at twelve to fourteen weeks, but this could change literally overnight if a puppy with a case of distemper was brought to him. So the motto must be to inform your vet when you first get your puppy, and be guided by him.

Most sensible breeders will worm puppies at an early stage, and you must check when you buy your dog whether this has been done, but worms are a particularly invidious parasite that your dog is likely to pick up throughout its life. There are two species of worm which infest dogs: tapeworms and roundworms. They are different in appearance and are easily recognised and identified. Roundworms are round and firm to the touch, looking like thin spaghetti, with tapered ends normally white or pale pink, and look very similar to long, thin, colourless earthworms. Puppies normally have to be treated for roundworms twice. If the breeder has already administered the first dose he will instruct you as to when the second dose is due. If not you must give both treatments yourself. You will see the dead worms being passed by the dog when he defecates. It is also advisable to treat your dog every six to eight weeks thereafter, until he is a year old.

The first signs of tapeworms are normally noticed as small white sections, either seen in the dog's faeces, or sticking around the hair at the dog's anus. With young dogs it is inadvisable to wait until you see the small segments in evidence. It is better to treat your dog on the assumption that he does have the parasite. The tapeworm, which can grow to quite astonishing lengths, is a creamy white colour, and much flatter than roundworms. It

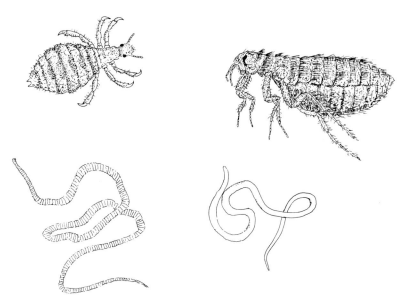

Parasites, *top left* louse, *top right* flea, *bottom left* tapeworm, *bottom right* roundworm.

is made up of segments, and throughout your dog's life, particularly if it is likely that he has been picking up bits of debris (such as pieces of dead rabbit) in the country, it is wise to give him an occasional treatment to eradicate any worms that may be there. Try to get into the habit of occasionally examining his faeces, breaking them open with a stick, and looking for tapeworm segments.

An alternative to occasionally dosing the dog and examining his faeces is to initially ensure that the dog is clear of intestinal parasites, and then to regularly feed him on the treatments available, such as Everfree. This should of course prevent further infestation. It is perhaps some comfort to know that canine tapeworms are not harmful to humans, neither can they be spread from one dog to another. A dog can only be infested with tapeworm if it eats a host animal, such as rabbit.

Ticks are no respecters of any mammal species and will happily attach themselves to any host – sheep, cattle, mink, stoats, deer, humans, cats, and of course, dogs. If you pick up a tick whilst in the country you'll probably notice it within a few hours, as its body fills with blood. Normally, feeling it rubbing against your clothing, you discover its presence and deal with it in the same manner as you would one on your dog. However, dogs must be checked regularly, particularly after visits to the country side, especially any areas where there is long grass, bracken or heather.

Ticks are either reddish-brown or grey and are picked up by a passing animal whilst the tick is in its deflated state. They then crawl on the host to the area of their choice, often in the soft areas behind the ears or groin, (but they can be found anywhere on a dog) where they burrow their heads in, and proceed to ingest the dog's blood. They can normally only be found in their swollen state. When running your hands and eyes over the dog, examining it carefully you will either see the tick, or sometimes feel it as a small bump imbedded in a thick coat. Their size can be quite alarming, some of them growing as large as a peanut, and they must be removed.

The best and simplest way to remove a tick from a dog is to carefully pick it away close to the skin. Occasionally, if the tick's head is left imbedded in the skin, the area can become infected and a small suppurating sore develops. So over the next few days, watch the area where you removed the tick to make sure that it clears up.

There are other methods of removing ticks, but these are largely dependent upon the site where the tick is fastened. One is to cover it with vaseline until it moves and it can be picked off. But it is not advised to hold a lit cigarette end to the tick. Whilst it might work on a human who can stop if it is burning him, a dog, if burnt in such a way would quickly prove unwilling to allow further investigations.

Few dogs escape an occasional infestation of fleas or lice, normally first noticed because your dog will start scratching furiously. If you examine the area where your dog is scratching, you may find the culprit. Lice, smaller than fleas, are grey and move about the host slowly, whereas fleas, normally 3mm long, are black and jump much more quickly than lice.

Whilst the infestation on the dog is a relatively simple matter to treat with a good canine delousing powder the infestation can pose the additional problem that the parasites may be very difficult to eradicate completely. If the dog is kennelled it requires the burning of his bedding and thorough disinfecting of the whole kennel, particularly the sleeping area. If he is a house dog, his bed should either be thoroughly washed or burnt, and the carpets vigorously cleaned. However, anyone who has fitted carpets must assume that at some time they will get fleas, since the little creatures love to live in the corners of the room, huddled together in the warmth of the fitted carpet. Once fleas have been brought in it is virtually impossible to guarantee their complete removal, but this should not worry the householder unduly, as they are just one of the many parasites that are part of every home in the country.

A dog which has had either fleas or lice will require two shampoo treatments, two weeks apart – the first to destroy the adults, the second to make sure that all the eggs have also been destroyed.

Mites are too small for you to see clearly with your naked eye. But these are the creatures that cause mange and allied conditions. Their presence normally heralds a general irritation of the skin, or infection of the ear, and if treated with a good canine delousing shampoo can be cured.

In summary then, it is well to remember the general guidelines about both, internal and external parasites: if they are not checked parasites will cause deterioration of your dog's physical condition and looks, and obviously the greater the infestation the more difficult it is to eradicate the problem. Yet none are serious if treated promptly, preferably after consultation with your vet.

DISEASES AND INOCULATIONS

The four principal diseases that dogs are most likely to contract in Britain are fortunately preventable through inoculation. But if not inoculated against, the result of infection in your dog can vary from the fairly serious to the fatal.

DISTEMPER AND HARDPAD

At one time thought to be different ailments, they are in fact the same disease, merely appearing in different guises. This horrific disease is caused by the virus invading the nervous system and is extremely serious. Even with modern veterinary medicines it is normally fatal.

INFECTIOUS HEPATITIS

In its initial stages this disease is often confused with distemper since they share similar symptoms of general listlessness, loss of appetite, high temperature, vomiting and diarrhoea. This illness is caused by germs infecting the liver.

LIVER LEPTOSPIROS (*Leptospira icterohaemorrhagica*)

This disease of the liver is sometimes spread by rats; can cause jaundice, and can be passed on to humans.

KIDNEY LEPTOSPIROSIS (*Leptospira canicola*)

In common with the other leptospiral diseases this is a disease which humans can contract. The kidney leptospirosis is carried in the dog's urine, and is normally particularly virulent anywhere where well-used lamp posts or urinal posts are to be found, such as in cities. The illness is often unnoticed it being assumed that the dog is just a little off colour for a short time, the owner being unaware that the dog has damaged kidneys which can prove fatal in later life.

Dog owners that live in the city are normally unaware of quite what a hive of infection lamp posts and areas where dog's urinate actually are; nor do they realise that any dog using such an infected site is giving the live virus with which it has been inoculated the effect of a booster, actually re-infecting the dog and keeping his protection to a maximum. It is wise if you live in the country where few dogs mix with your own, to occasionally take your dog to the city and walk him around on a lead, letting him sniff at a few lamp posts. This will have the effect of giving him the booster that city dogs enjoy all the time.

No matter how well inoculated your dog is, if he becomes unwell; going off his food, having diarrhoea, constipation, or acting below colour, if you cannot attribute the cause to any immediate reason, such as a dramatic change in diet or heavy unaccustomed exercise, the best advice is always to consult your vet. Don't be afraid of taking your dog to the vet if you are worried about him in any way. It is much better to have him treated in the early stages of a complaint, rather than wait until you feel more justified in bothering your vet. Your new puppy is like a small baby, and if he becomes ill he can deteriorate very quickly. Both your vet and your wallet will prefer early or preventive treatment rather than facing major problems later on.

Indeed, if you are having a minor problem with your dog, a simple telephone call to your vet's surgery can often put you on the right path. I have a very good relationship with my own local veterinary practice. If I am unsure of any aspect of my dogs' health I have no hesitation in getting in touch with the vet to ask for his help, and I have been working with dogs for over twenty years.

The behavioural pattern of your dog starts off with the first formative experiences he has of you, his surroundings, and his world in general, and there is much that you can do with a young puppy to lay a strong basic foundation in your relationship that will greatly help in his future training. First of all he must have confidence in you, so whenever you are with him be gentle, speak kindly to him, encourage his confidence, give him a pat of acknowledgement when he runs to you. Then, when you take him outdoors for the first few times he will be able to view the world with a great deal more assurance, since he will be with you, and you after all have taken the place of both his mother and the pack leader.

An example of this is with a young puppy that strays away from you, perhaps thirty yards, and meets something that causes him fright or alarm. What does he do but immediately yelp and run back to you. He runs to you because he has confidence in you to protect and defend him.

Once your puppy is confident in your company, you can try early training. Part of that is the house-training previously mentioned which is the beginnings of discipline. Another aspect of his very early training is in the recognition of his name. Other early training is to make a little dummy. What I use is a little roll of leather, easily carried, but with no surfaces that a pup's needle-like teeth can snag on. I throw the dummy across the floor, and encourage the puppy to bring it to me. Often you can find with young puppies if they pick it up at all, they dash off with it, wanting to play. It is best simply to retrieve the dummy from the dog, put it away and forget about it for another week or so, whilst you concentrate on occasionally calling the dog to you, making him familiar with his name. When he comes to you, stroke him, talk to him and show him that you appreciate him coming to you. Whatever you do, never be tempted to run after the puppy to retrieve your dummy. The game of 'chases' is one that all young puppies love to play, and if either your or any of your family allow him to indulge in it you may as well give up the whole idea of making him into a retriever, no matter what breed he is, for if he gets it into his head that carrying things in his mouth means running off with someone trying to catch him, how are you going to rearrange his mind to think exactly the opposite – that carrying anything in his mouth means bringing it back to you?

After he comes to you readily at the call of his name, you can try the small dummy technique again. Don't be concerned or alarmed if he persists in wanting to play with it, just take it from him and ignore the event. Some puppies can take a long time before the idea occurs to them that they should bring the dummy to you. But whatever you do, *don't chase him.*

SITTING

Of all the commands that any gundog is ever likely to receive, none is more important or has a greater influence on all other aspects of his training than sitting. The command to sit, whether by voice, whistle, hand, shot or flushed game, is of vital importance in his future life and must bring about an automatic response, so it is imperative that he is introduced to this particular task early on, and that he learns to do it crisply and willingly. Sitting is the ultimate foundation stone of all discipline training, since it is simple – if you cannot make him sit you will not successfully be able to move on to any other of the many tasks you may require of him.

Sitting means that the dog stops whatever activity it is involved in, or is about to become involved in. A dog that will sit instantly on command will not run away from you, chase rabbits, or pursue other dogs. The dog will sit where he has been told when you are busy with something else. For the shooting man the command to sit also means 'stop and look at me, you're going the wrong way and I want to give you directions'. When a dog is sitting he is under your control. Yet so often this simple to teach, utterly important command is sloppy and performed at the dog's convenience, a sure sign that the handler has not put sufficient emphasis on this fundamental command.

Introducing your young dog to the act of sitting is as simple as this – hold his food bowl in one hand, above his head. With the other hand push his bottom into a sitting position, and gently, but firmly and clearly say the word 'sit'. Hold him in that position for a very short time, perhaps as long as it takes you to slowly count to five, then let him go with the words 'take it'.

Sitting to flush.

Once your dog is happily sitting on the touch of your hand, combined with your voice, then it is time for you to start gently taking your hand away, ever ready if he makes towards the food bowl to gently restrain him by putting one hand on his chest and the other on his haunches, and put him into the sitting position with the firm command 'sit'.

While he is learning this particular lesson, you should be extending the time you hold him in the sitting position before telling him to 'take it'. If this particular early training is done gently, over a period of two or three weeks, you will find that you can move from squatting beside him to standing with the bowl between you at your feet while he sits patiently waiting for you to allow him to eat.

Once the young puppy starts to sit confidently and comfortably on command, start to raise your right arm, palm downward, in a Nazi-style salute, when you command him to sit. Standing in front of him, gently tell him to sit whilst holding your arm in the air. The dog from this early age will get used to the picture of you standing with your arm in the air as he sits. He will in the weeks and months to follow, use this as a purely visual command, but remember when giving the sitting hand signal, always to keep your arm well above your shoulder, since the dog sees only your silhouette, and a hand held in front of your body cannot be seen at a distance.

INTRODUCTION TO THE LEAD

Introducing a small puppy to the lead can be as easy as just fitting it and walking on – almost as though the dog already knew what was expected of him, or it can have the opposite effect. Some young dogs, when they first feel the restriction of the lead, will buck and plunge, jerk, squeal, or sometimes stand motionless and absolutely rigid. But whatever the reaction of his first introduction, the treatment is exactly the same, and must be done at an early age, otherwise you will have no way of either restraining your dog or keeping it in control when you take it outdoors.

When you are first going to fit the lead to your pup, squat down beside him, stroke him, speak gently to him, fit the lead and walk on. If he starts to buck and plunge you must use your intelligence and give the dog a combination of gentle encouragement, while at the same time dragging him by the rope. Even the worst cases I have encountered will very quickly accept the lead, and happily walk with you when it is fitted.

It is of great importance that up until the age of six months you restrain yourself from requiring too much of a puppy. You must remember that you are training a dog, you are not in a race, and the timings given in this book and all others are merely guidelines of what to expect at a particular age. But all dogs are individuals and have completely different personalities. Therefore what one dog will find easy to learn and pick up, another individual may take longer to grasp. Apart from house-training, early manners and sitting, it is best just to enjoy your puppy, and let him enjoy his puppyhood during these early months.

4. SIX TO NINE MONTHS

There is no magic day in the calendar when your dog should start his training. Some individuals are steadier, quieter, and give the impression of being keen to learn earlier than others, but most dogs should be ready to start their early training between six and seven months, whilst others may not be ready until they are eight or nine months old.

Throughout all gundog training, every task, lesson, or command ever given to your dog, hinges on one foundation stone, that of discipline. Without your dog being disciplined and under your command and control you can do nothing. So an early discipline training is vital, making him aware of your voice, and introducing him to the pleasures of working with you. Without working continually on these very basic discipline exercises you will allow your young dog to develop bad habits, and like all habits, once they start they are virtually impossible to eradicate. Most faults found in adult dogs can be traced back to shoddy discipline work in their early formative months of training. So *at all times* you must be in control of the dog, and never allow him to forget that.

Whilst I maintain that there is no mystique in training a gundog, and that anyone with a modicum of common-sense can turn out an impeccable dog, there is one aspect of working with a young dog that is absolutely vital. It is so important to the future success of a potential gundog, that unless you, the trainer and handler are able to examine your own personality and can say with absolute confidence that you have that particular ingredient within yourself, you would be better to send your dog to a professional kennel for training. The ingredient I refer to is *patience*. You must never lose your patience when you are training your dog, even if he does not seem to be able to grasp a particular lesson for the moment. Everyone, including dogs, can have off days, and if you feel you are in danger of becoming frustrated and annoyed with your dog it is better to stop your training session and return home. If you try to continue under these circumstances you can do irrevocable damage to the 'special' relationship you are trying to build up with your dog.

It should never be necessary to shout at your dog. If he does not obey the command given in a normal tone of voice, there is no reason for him to obey you when you bawl at him. Even worse, you are creating a precedent in his mind – if he gets used to the shouted command he will never obey the spoken command. Dogs have excellent hearing, so there is absolutely no reason for you to strain your vocal chords in an effort to make him obey. A quietly spoken but *firm* word is all that is required.

Another aspect of training your dog which I must emphasise at this stage is the avoidance of boredom, brought on by repetition. Not only will the dog cease to enjoy his work, but he will begin to anticipate your commands. For example, if you always go to the same spot, throw the same dummy in the same place, and send him to retrieve it, you will soon find that before the dummy has left your hand the dog has raced off to the spot where it is expected to land, so that he can bring it back to you. If you make every part of his training simple and fun, you should find few problems with him. Enjoyment is the key to much of his training – all working dogs must enjoy what they are doing, particularly if, as in the case of gundogs, they are required to use their brains, and to perform for you. If they do not enjoy the tasks put forward for them, they will not do them, it is as simple as that.

Your dog will by now sit nicely on command, having been gently introduced to this particular task over the preceding months, using his feeding bowl as an aid. He should sit on the command 'sit' or by hand signal, his response being almost automatic.

When you take your dog out for a training session, whether you live in the country or the city and whether you can walk or must drive to the area where you are going to train your dog, it is imperative that you first let him relieve himself. If there are rabbits likely to be on your ground then it is better to walk them off the area you intend to work your dog before you start. If your young dog spots and then chases a rabbit that is still on the ground, call him back, but under no circumstances chastise him for this. He is young and untrained, and does not yet know that such things are forbidden. If you do beat him you may just be planting the seed in his mind that picking rabbits up equals a beating, and he will refuse to pick game from then on. Just make sure that such accidents do not happen again.

WALKING TO HEEL

The first few weeks when a small puppy is fitted to a lead it is normally sufficient just to use it as a restraint to keep him with you, but as he gets used to it, you can start to introduce him to the 'heel' command. Personally, I prefer not to start giving this command until the dog is six months old, using the lead up until this point purely as a way of attaching him to me.

The heel command is simplicity in itself. When you decide to introduce it fit the lead and with it slack, let the dog stray forward, then firmly jerk him back into position as you say the word 'heel'. Normally if this is repeated on two or three occasions the dog quickly learns to pace himself and walk beside you, rather than stray forward and get what he knows will be a sharp jerk back. Firmness in this particular command will save many later problems, for it is better for your dog to endure three or four hard and sharp jerks, rather than numerous apologetic ones that he will soon get used to and then ignore.

The alternative way of introducing this command is to carry with you a light switch, and swing it like a pendulum as you walk, so that it passes in front of the dog's face, which will have the natural effect of making him walk in position. Unfortunately it can, with some dogs, create the problem of making him walk out from you, and I don't advise it at this early stage. Better just to jerk him back into position when necessary, and make him walk with his head on a level with your knee, or even a pace behind you, but not in front, since later we will introduce him to sitting when you stop, and if his head is in front of you, he will be less able, either to pace himself to your speed, or to see when you stop walking.

When you are quite confident that your dog understands and obeys the 'heel' command you can make him walk to heel without the lead. Because you have always kept him on a slack lead when walking you should simply remove the lead from the dog, repeat the word 'heel' and he should walk on beside you as before. From that point on, whenever you take your dog for a walk alternate walking with the lead and without it for short periods. However, don't be tempted at this stage, remembering he is still very much a puppy, to try walking him without the lead where he is likely to encounter distractions such as people, other dogs, rabbits, etc. It is really asking too much of the dog to inflict that sort of discipline yet.

THE FIRST TRAINING SESSIONS

Put your dog on the lead, and this applies to all breeds, walk him nicely to heel in a zig-zag line, whilst you vary the pace at which you walk. This makes the dog aware of your speed and he will vary his speed accordingly, since he must pace himself to keep up with you, never the other way around. Take the lead off the dog and continue walking him to heel for a short distance before commanding him to sit. Stand in front of the dog, and with your arm raised in a Nazi-style salute, keep him in the sitting position, and take a few slow paces backwards, always ready to go forward and command him to sit as you gently push him back into position, if he stands up. If he creeps forward, return to him, firmly drag him back to the position you had left him sitting in, and push him firmly down, whilst saying the word 'sit', then again walk backwards. On these first few occasions, you should be aiming to get about twenty feet away from him. Stand there, count up to ten slowly, and then go back to the dog, and keeping him sitting, pat his head, gently praising him

If your dog is walking nicely to heel at this stage, stand beside him, and patting your left thigh, speak his name, and walk on with him to heel. If he has not yet walked to heel without the lead, fit it and walk on with him to heel. Walk in a zig-zag course, stopping every now and again, always giving him the command to sit when you stop. The whole idea in this early discipline training is to make the dog aware of his speed being in direct relation to your pace, and to bind him to walking with you, sitting when you stop, and remaining sat until you tell him to heel. In any one training exercise period, you should try to leave him sat on three separate positions. An example of this would be - walk him to heel, make him sit when you stop, walk a few yards away, return to him and pat your thigh with your left hand and speak his name. Walk on with the dog, stop, command him to sit, stand beside him for a few minutes, then pat your thigh, speak his name and walk on with him. Stop, command him to sit, and repeating the word 'sit' – walk a few yards away from him. Wait for a minute and return to him, pat your thigh, speak his name and walk on. Keep practising this particular exercise, continually stretching the distance between you and your sitting dog and the time you leave him sitting before you return. Most dogs quickly get into the routine once they understand what is expected of them.

All training, as I have said, hinges on your ability to quietly and gently control your dog, and to have him at all times under your control. You cannot move to any other form of training until the dog will sit nicely to command.

It is of the utmost importance that in five out of six times when you leave a dog in the sitting position and walk away from it, that you return to it, and only one in six do you call him to you. The reason is simply this: when a dog is left in a sitting position, it should be content and happy to remain there, not expecting or anticipating the handler to call it. If a dog is left sitting and you walk away, always to return, the dog will not become anxious, and will not be sitting there prepared to explode into action as soon as you make the slightest sound or smallest movement. On the one in six occasions when you call your dog to you, pat your right thigh with a straight right arm and use big arm movements so the dog gets used to the visual command as you call his name and encourage him to come to you.

SITTING TO WHISTLE

Once he sits to voice, you can then start to add variations. Leaving the dog in a sitting position, walk thirty yards away and call him to you. As he is running towards you, give him the command to sit, whilst throwing your right arm in the air (as previously described). He may sit immediately, or more likely will slow down and come forward more hesitantly. Sharply command him to sit. If he keeps coming right up to you before he sits, firmly drag him back to where he was when you commanded him to sit, make him sit, then repeat the exercise. Once your dog masters this particular lesson you should be able to leave him sitting, walk away, call him to you, stop him half way (using both voice and hand) then call him to you again, this time right up to your feet, where you should make a fuss of him for being a good dog.

Now is the time to introduce the whistle. There are many good whistles on the market, but the one that I recommend and use myself is the simple, inexpensive, buffalo horn whistle. I do not have much use for the silent whistle, since I like to be able to modulate the tone to my own ear.

With your dog on the lead, walk around the training ground, command him to sit as you stop, while at the same time give your whistle a single toot. He will sit because he recognised the verbal command, and he should be well used to sitting whenever you stop. At first the whistle command will be simply just another sound, yet very shortly he will come to associate the act of sitting with the sound of the whistle, and the whistle will then have taken on the function of being a separate command. However, it is best in the initial training of a young dog, when you add in a new command to sit, to add it to the already familiar command of voice or hand. For instance, when you leave him sitting in front of you and walk away, call him to you and command him to sit, and as you command him to sit, throw your right arm in the air, and give the whistle a toot. Do not be timid with your whistle, give a good loud blast on it. You want to make sure that the dog has a clear understanding of the sound, and eventually you will be expecting him to obey the whistle command from a considerable distance away, so start the way you will have to continue, and don't be afraid to make a noise.

By practice alone, the dog will soon drop at the sound of the whistle, and you will discover that, almost without trying, your dog will be able to sit to all three commands. You can then start adding in variations of the three. Try calling him to you and command him to sit to hand and whistle, without the spoken command. Once this is successfully accomplished you can then start calling him to you and use the whistle alone to make him stop. In this way, over the next few months, you will continue to build up the dog's versatility with the command to sit.

Up until now your dog will have come to you either at a hand signal (pat of the right thigh), a verbal command (calling his name), or more usually at this stage, a combination of both. He will only have heard the whistle as a command to sit. Once he has become familiar and totally responsive to these commands, you can add in the whistle recall.

Tin of blanks and dog whistle.

This is easily done by leaving the dog sitting, walking away from him, and when you call him to you, pat your thigh and give your whistle several loud short toots. At first the dog, on hearing the whistle, may either slow down or stop, but you must encourage him on, crouching down to make yourself look less imposing to the dog, and he should soon learn the difference between a single whistle command to sit – tooooot – and several, which is the signal to return to you – toot, toot, toot, toot. When he returns to you, always acknowledge the fact that you are happy with him by praising him.

This early basic discipline training can be greatly enhanced if you remember always to vary the commands as much as possible. Also important is never spending too long in one training session and watch the dog for signs of disinterest or boredom. It is far more beneficial to your dog, and potentially less frustrating for you, if you try to spend half an hour every evening when you are training him, rather than leaving it until the weekend and giving him an intensive one or two day session. That will almost certainly lead both of you to boredom and sloppiness. If there is absolutely no way you can take your dog out during the week – it may be dark by the time you return home from your work – then obviously you will have to make do with weekend training periods. But even then spend no more than one hour teaching your dog, particularly at this initial stage of his training.

You should now be able to walk out with your dog at heel, on or off the lead, have him sit when you stop and remain where he is on the command to sit whilst you walk on, allowing you to get progressively further and further away before five out of six times you return to him. He should dash toward you on a verbal, visual, or whistle command, and stop and sit to a verbal, visual or whistle command, delivered together or separately. This early discipline, if approached gently but firmly, and got absolutely right is, as I have said, one of the main foundation stones of all your dog's training and general discipline in years to come.

EARLY RETRIEVING

Simultaneous to the discipline training of your dog, you can introduce him to retrieving. Again, the correct time to start him on retrieving depends very much on the dog, and if you find that when you throw a retrieve the dog shows no interest, then it is best to put the dummy away and not try again for perhaps another week. For the initial introduction of your dog to a dummy you can either purchase a lightweight dog-training dummy from any gun shop, or even better at this stage make one up yourself, in scale to the size of puppy you have. If you have a small light breed, then a dummy constructed of a washing-up liquid container inside a couple of old socks firmly bound is normally sufficient.

When you go out to start your exercise period with your dog, throw the dummy a few yards in front of him, and encourage him to run for it, with the command 'fetch', using an exaggerated arm movement in that direction as you give the command. It is worthwile mentioning at this early stage that whenever you throw a dummy out for your dog to retrieve, try always to throw it into the wind, getting him used to the awareness of the scent, as he goes for the dummy. It will be a while before he stops relying on his eyes and starts educating his nose, but using the wind now will help to encourage him, and discipline yourself to be aware of wind direction.

With luck, your dog will immediately dash out, grab the

Greylag geese in a turnip field.

dummy and then run back to you. As he does this, you must give him much praise and make a fuss of him. If he runs off with the dummy, don't worry, turn and run away from him, calling him to you. If he is reluctant to come to you, squat down, making yourself as small as possible, and encourage him to you, then when he comes up to you make a great fuss before gently removing the dummy from his mouth. One retrieve in any training session is sufficient. What is of greater importance is the fact that he picks it up.

When your dog understands that he is expected to retrieve, you can start restraining his behaviour by making him sit for longer and longer periods of time before you allow him to retrieve the dummy. Tell him to sit and throw the dummy. If he lunges forward eagerly, repeat the sit command, holding on to the dog if necessary. Count to ten slowly and allow him to retrieve. If the sit command has been well learnt this should pose no problem, and the dog should soon wait for your command to 'fetch' before he dashes after the dummy. However all dogs are different, some may be able to control themselves easily and be quite happy to sit until told otherwise, whilst other excitable animals will get themselves into a real state as they try desperately to control their urge to move. The excitable dogs should be eased into the exercise more slowly, taking longer until they can be left for the same length of time as their more placid mates.

When you send your young dog on a retrieve, try to remember to repeat the word 'steady' as he nears the dummy. Although at this stage he should be able to see the dummy, in his later training, particularly with blind retrieves, when he hears his handler saying 'steady' once or twice he will know he is in the right area for finding the retrieve.

It is of great help to your dog, if, when you send him on a retrieve which is blind you can line him up, giving him the line and direction in which he should run. This is easily done if introduced at an early age on visual retrieves. Throw the dummy where the dog can see it, then crouch down beside him, stroke him, and put your arm straight out in a pointing action toward the retrieve, almost as though you were lining the dog up, and then send him out. With practice, on all retrieves where you send the dog from a position beside you, if you get into the habit of squatting down and lining him up, he will naturally start to take the line of your arm.

The transference of line direction, when you come to blind retrieves, will then be a natural thing. He will by now subconsciously have got it into his head to run straight out the way you are pointing him and with the experience of having found the seen retrieve will naturally go straight out in the direction that you indicate.

When you have first introduced a young dog to a retrieve, and he has successfully dashed out and picked it up, you must restrain yourself from giving him just one more. Throughout his life the dog must never get the idea that any retrieve, whatever it is, whether a thrown dummy, one shot from a dummy launcher, or a dead bird, is his property, which he can automatically dash after. He must always remain under your control, and the easiest way of teaching him this is simply to pick up most of the retrieves yourself.

Go about it in the following simple fashion: leave him sitting, squat beside him and throw the dummy a few yards, telling him to sit as you throw the dummy. Restrain him if he tries to dash after it, commanding him to sit, then go forward and pick the dummy yourself. In any training exercise period it is permissible at first to throw three retrieves which you yourself collect, but never more than one in any training period that the dog is allowed to go for. Later, as we advance his training, we will increase the number of retrieves that he collects, but not until his training is more advanced will he get more than two in a session.

You may find that when your young dog dashes out and picks up a retrieve that he does so enthusiastically, but is reluctant either to give it up or bring it back, and a common problem many trainers find is the dog running around them in a wide arc. This can be avoided if you stand against a wall or a fence, and squat down, until the dog is quite confident and happy to run back to you, carrying the retrieve, and holding it up for you to take from his mouth. Never snatch it out of his mouth.

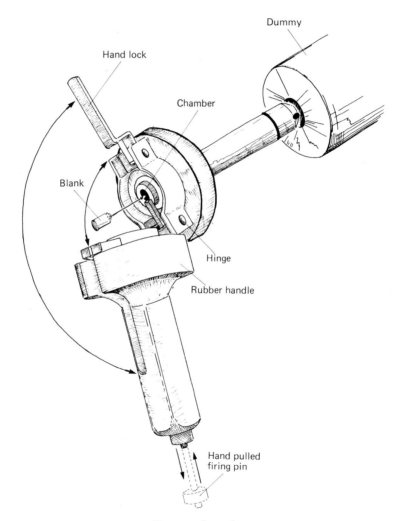

Dummy launcher.

Put your hand under his chin and hold the dummy in his mouth for a few seconds before gently removing it with the word 'dead'. Although if a dog was trialing the handler would wish to remove the retrieve from the dog's mouth as quickly as possible, in the shooting field the situation can often be slightly different. I like to get my dogs used to holding the retrieve for a short time before I take it from them, saying 'dead' at all times, as the command for them to spit it out. This means that there is never any danger of the dog spitting the retrieve out as soon as he reaches me and before I am ready to take it. How many shooting men have lost runners in this way? Conversely however, if your particular dog is so keen that he is, at this stage, reluctant to hold on to the dummy in his willingness to get on to the next exercise, take the dummy from him as soon as he gets back to you. It is far better to make him always give it to hand than to risk him dropping the retrieve on the ground.

Between the ages of six to nine months, with the exception of the introduction to water which I will come to later, you should concentrate on the basic discipline, as I have outlined, of sitting to command, coming to you and stopping on command, intermixed. To prevent boredom mix this with throwing retrieves, which you go for three times out of four. Until all these exercises can be done to perfection, there is no point in moving on to any more-advanced lessons.

INTRODUCTION TO WATER

Like every other part of any young dog's training in his formative months, the introduction to water is very largely dependent upon how much confidence the young dog has in you, the handler. A young dog is not going to respond in any type of training if he is either frightened of you or unsure of your actions, so when you come to introducing him to water, you must approach this potentially frightening new type of environment with great care on the assumption that he may well be afraid of it. Then, if you discover that he rushes up and dives in without fuss, that's a bonus. But approach all young dogs with the attitude that they are likely to be afraid.

Pick a warm day. If you have access to an older dog which is used to swimming, so much the better. With a pair of wellingtons or waders, take your young dog to a pond, or slowly moving stream. If you have an older dog with you the pup will often follow him into the shallows. But it is better for you to

Flighting out in evening, returning to water roost.

go into the water yourself and encourage the young dog in. If he is reluctant, postpone the introduction for another week. I have never known any of the retrieving gundog breeds not to enjoy swimming, although some dogs certainly are more reluctant to first enter water than others. Whatever you do, you must in no way force the dog to enter the water, and never be tempted to throw him in. Take your time and you will find that a gentle introduction will be much more beneficial in the end. Swimming is after all great fun for most dogs, but just like humans, they must gain confidence before they can be expected to dive in with gay abandon.

REWARD AND PUNISHMENT

There can be no better advice for any gundog owner who wants to get really good results from training his young dog than to establish a loving, happy relationship with the dog during its formative months or childhood. Play with it as often as you can, take it for walks, indulge it, give it confidence in you. Try never to raise your voice, shout, or frighten your young dog, for I have never met any dog of any breed that does not respond well to a loving owner. By indulgence and affection I do not mean softness. It will be necessary for you to chastise your young dog at different times in his career, but it is best effected by a firm voice. When discipline is needed, intelligence must prevail, for once a dog becomes afraid of you, you are well on your way to losing it. So try to strike the balance and command respect through obedience and affection, rather than chastisement and threats.

The idea of offering a gundog a reward as an aid in training is completely taboo to some authorities on the subject. Although I would never introduce a 'circus-type' reward for tricks performed, I can see no harm in the *rare* titbit to help you over a thorny problem with your dog. For example, if your young dog, even after many sessions, is totally unwilling to bring a dummy straight back to you, preferring instead to run about with it happily in his mouth, then it may be that all he needs is the inducement of a doggy biscuit to bring him running back to you. A bit of bribery will help you over the hurdle. Once over the other side you can put the biscuits away. As long as you use the reward method very occasionally you should have no worries with it. If a reward is given too often the dog will become sloppy in his performance because of his keeness to return to you for the expected titbit. Another advantage in being open to giving your dog a reward is when, for whatever reason, your dog has lost confidence in you. It may be that you unfortunately lost your temper with him, or even another member of the family did, and the dog has become reluctant to come to you. A small treat produced from your pocket can often bring the confidence surging back.

The subject of chastisement is also a difficult one, and must be approached with intelligence and caution. A dog has no memory for crimes committed hours previously. No matter how angry you are at a torn shoe or chewed carpet, any more than showing the dog the crime and a firm 'no' is pointless. You must stop the dog in the act to be effective. As far as the thorny question of hitting is concerned, a dog taken by the scruff of the neck, shaken, with the word 'no' firmly said, is normally punished sufficiently. For more serious and immediate chastisement, either a rolled newspaper, or the open palm of your hand is all that is needed, for one must remember that to administer pain to a dog is ineffectual. It is your displeasure, causing fear of you, that will bring results. The whacking with a rolled newspaper combines discomfort and noise, and is much more effective, for instance, than hitting with a stick.

The whole business of knowing exactly how much punishment to administer often confuses people. A gentleman once brought a dog to me, to see if I could make any improvements in him. He introduced himself and immediately went on to explain that his large and very handsome black labrador dog was running rings around him. He continued by telling me that he had beaten the dog until his hands were sore, and kicked him until he had actually hurt his foot. Needless to say, the dog was beyond help because he assumed that all forms of chastisment for all crimes were the same – a roaring voice and a beating. The dog had become immune to punishment.

There is also the example of another labrador that was brought to my kennels for training. It arrived sitting comfortably on the lap of the owner's wife, who could barely be seen, as she peered out from behind the bulk of the very large dog she was cradling like a child. In due course, a few months later the dog was collected by his owner. The dog was fully trained and an excellent working dog. It was demonstrated to him, and off he went, highly satisfied. Yet a few weeks later the owner was on the telephone full of tales of woe about his dog running in and generally running wild.

I asked him to bring it back to that I could see for myself this amazing turn around in a dog that had only recently left my hands, well trained. True enough, when we went out into the field, the dog would pay no attention to its owner as it ran this way and that. He shot a dummy for the dog, using my dummy launcher, and the dog was after it in a flash, ignoring his shouting and blowing of the whistle. I, who had been sitting in the car, watching this, trying not to let the dog realise I was there, got out and called the dog over. I clipped him on the ear, told him to walk to heel, and off we set. As if by magic the dog began to behave himself perfectly, sitting when I stopped, and when I shot a dummy, sitting patiently while I collected it. Then I shot another which the dog retrieved beautifully to hand on command. The owner, as you can imagine, was quite astonished at this. What, he enquired, was the reason for such different behaviour? Brutally I told him the dog had realised that he was a mug. Knowing it would get away with it, it had been allowed to do as it pleased, and was happy to do so. I gave the owner a lesson in how and when to administer discipline, pointing out to him that he had no alternative, unless he wished the dog to completely take over and make a fool of him, and off he went. He telephoned me a few weeks later to report that the dog was doing extremely well, the problems had disappeared. A perfect example of a man whose attitude was too soft.

I had another good example – a beautiful flatcoated retriever bitch who came in for training. She walked to heel well, pacing herself to the speed I walked at during training sessions, was well-mannered, and happily sat immediately I stopped. Yet when the same dog went out for a walk with its owner, a young woman who lives nearby, it immediately started to play up. The only experience it had with the young woman was one of playful indulgence and when walking to heel on the lead the dog continually walked with its head and neck bent in front of her legs, looking up at her, causing her to either bump into the dog, or trip and stumble. Rather than forcibly jerking the dog back into the heel position, she was more likely to give her an apologetic tug, which was a momentary inconvenience to the dog. When this dog sat at my feet when I stopped it sat to one side as she had been trained, and patiently looked about. When the owner asked the dog to do the same thing she would not sit patiently, and continually jumped to her feet, wagging her tail, wanting to play.

It is often said that there is no such thing as a bad dog, only bad owners, and this is very true, for irrespective of how well trained a young dog is it is the owner's attitude that governs the dog's behaviour. So it is absolutely imperative, whenever you are training a dog, to fully realise the importance of achieving a balance of respect and affection, and not to have a soft attitude, crediting the dog with human emotions or intelligence. Rather remember that a dog will take its lead from the attitude of its owner, and consistency is imperative at all times.

Before moving on to the next stage in the training of your dog it is worthwhile reiterating that you are not in a race, so have patience with your dog; time is very much on your side. If your dog is nine months old now but you are nowhere near the levels suggested in this chapter, do not rush him along in order to catch up. By the same token do not take things so slowly that your young dog is fast losing interest in the whole affair. If you are having a problem with any aspect of the training to date, stand back from it, and look at the problem with an objective eye, go back to square one and work the problem through. Your intelligence is far greater than the dog's so use it, outsmart him when you feel it necessary, trick him into resolving the problems. Don't skim over the surface and assume that these troubles will go away as the dog gets older. They won't. You and your dog together must resolve the problems. Use your common-sense, now and always when training your dog, and you should find that things will go smoothly – in the end.

5. NINE TO TWELVE MONTHS

Before every phase of training, it is an excellent idea to continually appraise the progress of your young dog by setting aside the occasional day when you run through all the training that has been achieved to date, rather than going out with the idea of training and practising what has already been taught on the same day.

Mallard drake.

Go to your normal training ground and run through everything you have done with your dog so far, giving him a minimum of commands, and those that you do, give quietly and directly. Walk him to heel on the lead. When you stop he should sit, at the pat of a thigh and his spoken name he should walk on with you. With the lead off he should walk to heel, sitting when you stop, and should remain where you have left him on the additional command of sit, allowing you to walk on as far as you wish, before you turn and walk back to him. Collecting him, he should again walk nicely to heel. He should sit on command to voice, whistle, or hand, whether he is running towards you or going away, and allow you to throw dummies all round him, which you then pick up. He should also happily retrieve whichever dummy you tell him to fetch, bringing it nicely to hand. And he should have been introduced to the delights of water.

This early part of your dog's training is, as I have said, the foundation stone on which you will build all his work training. Without a good, solid, confident obedience at this stage, it is pointless to go on. You can happily polish and hone your dog's abilities over the next year or so until he is absolutely superb – but only if these early training routines are firmly imbedded in the dog's head and his reactions are crisp and perfect. Any deviation or slackness at this stage is not acceptable and must be perfected before you move on, since if a dog does not have a firm grasp of everything that is expected of him so far, then the rest of his training will be built on shaky ground. Everything else you are going to train the dog to do are refinements and extensions of all this early training.

INTRODUCTION TO FEATHERED DUMMY

Up until now your dog will have retrieved only washing-up liquid dummies or canvas covered ones. Now you are about to add a new and more exciting dimension, that of the feathered dummy, and if done correctly this normally goes off without any fuss whatsoever. But as with all other aspects of training a dog, when you are introducing it to a new experience you must assume that things will not go perfectly, and never take anything for granted.

The best type of feathered dummy is made up of a light canvas dummy, with two closed pheasant's wings firmly bound on either side. Take your dog to your normal training area, throw one normal dummy and send the dog on a retrieve. He will, as he has been used to doing, dash out, grab the dummy and bring it to hand. Leave him in a sitting position, immediately throw the feathered dummy into the wind and send him

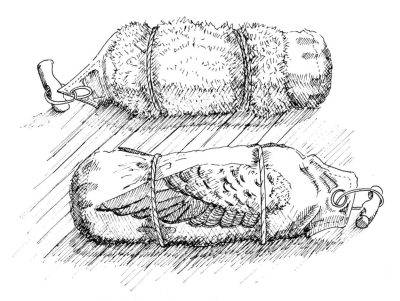

Hand dummies, one fur, one feather.

for it with the fetch command. As he nears it, encourage him on with it, calling 'steady' and when he picks the dummy shout, 'good boy, good boy' or similar encouraging noises. Very often, if approached in this way, you will discover that he rushes out and grabs the dummy, totally unaware of either its different texture or consistency, and will run back to you. If this is the case, then his introduction to the feathered dummy will have been effected without fuss, and from now on, all dummies should be feathered ones.

However, it is entirely possible that when he reaches the dummy he will either immediately be aware that the smell is different, or that the feel in his mouth is different. It is unlikely that any dog which is used to picking up a canvas dummy would refuse to pick it up, particularly if as he is approaching it you give him encouragement. If he does refuse to pick it, put it away, and don't try him on a feathered dummy for at least another week. Then try him on the feathered dummy at weekly intervals until he eventually picks it.

A more likely problem is that of the dog running back towards you with the feathered dummy, shaking it vigorously, or appearing reluctant to bring it straight to you. If there is any reluctance, immediately squat down, calling him on, or alternatively run backwards from him and when he does bring the retrieve to you, give him much praise.

If he grabs the dummy and starts to shake it, employ exactly the same tactics by encouraging him on, getting him to run after you, and take the dummy from him as soon as you can. Problems with the introduction to the feathered dummy normally solve themselves by a combination of familiarity of this new type of dummy, and by the simple expedient of taking a week before asking the dog to pick up the feathered dummy again. However, in my experience, any problems encountered at this stage are purely temporary, and with a little patience will go away. Whatever you do, no matter how frustrating you feel the whole situation is, particularly if the dog seems reluctant to return to you with the dummy, do not chase him and do not chastise him. Gently encourage him, and when he does bring the dummy to you, make a big fuss of him.

After your dog is converted to retrieving the feathered dummy, introduce him to the fur dummy, simply made by taking a piece of dried rabbit skin and binding it firmly around your canvas dummy. Then using exactly the same technique employed when introducing him to the feathered dummy, throw the by now familiar feathered dummy for a first retrieve, immediately followed by the fur dummy. The technique for solving any problems that may crop up is exactly the same as before.

Once you have your dog retrieving the fur or feathered dummy, continually ring the changes. Whilst it is never a good idea to give a dog too many retrieves in any one training exercise, you can by now get him up to two retrieves per training period, with occasional three retrieves, always endeavouring to mix the texture of the retrieves you want him to pick.

Remember, in all retrieving exercises the golden rule is that for every retrieve you throw for your dog, you must have thrown three which you yourself have retrieved, while he sits patiently watching you. You must avoid at all costs any dog getting it into his head that a retrieve is automatically his property, otherwise you are encouraging the crime of running in, chasing game, and generally being unsteady. Throughout his life, he must always regard any retrieve on which he is sent as a privilege, as a reward, but never as either his right or that the retrieve is his property.

INTRODUCTION TO SHOT

It is quite surprising how many people think that the idea of introducing a dog to shot is simply a matter of taking a very small puppy, firing a gun directly over its head, and finding out if he is afraid! Such techniques are not only extremely foolish but can cause problems that did not exist until such an action put them there. The sudden and unexpected terrifyingly loud bang from a shotgun, fired at close range at a young dog that has never heard such a sound before, can virtually frighten it out of its wits, make it flinch, and cause it to view a gun as an instrument of fright every time it appears. Therefore the introduction to shot should always follow exactly the same routine.

Snipe.

Enlist the aid of a friend, and get him to walk 100 yards or so away. Sit beside your dog, talking to it and comforting it. On a pre-arranged signal from you your companion should fire a shot in the air using a starting pistol. Watch your dog and give him encouragement. The dog will obviously react to the shot, in that he will turn his head and look in the direction from where it came. Have your friend fire another shot, while you make a fuss of your dog. Then progressively, your companion should come twenty paces closer before firing another shot at your hand signal. Continue in this way. Watch your dog carefully. If he shows any sign of fear, stop the lesson immediately and start again a few days later.

Dogs fall into three distinct categories when it comes to a shot being fired. Those to whom it means absolutely nothing and who will eventually learn to regard the shot as heralding a likely retrieve; those that are gun nervous and are disconcerted at the bang and will require a much longer introductory period to instil the confidence in them that there is nothing to be alarmed about; and those who are gun shy, which is a problem that cannot be solved.

Gun shyness is inherited, and must not be confused with the caution and trepidation which gun nervousness shows. A gun shy dog will just simply never come to terms with the noise of a gun, and in fact, they will quickly get to recognise the gun as the creator of this terrible noise, and many will run at the sight of the gun without a shot being fired. A gun shy dog will either cower timidly against your legs at the sound of a shot, or more normally will run away, either standing a distance off from you, quaking in fear or will often take to his heels, and ignoring your calls, run either all the way to your car, or back home.

It makes no sense whatsoever to keep a gun shy dog. It will never make a gundog, and the best advice for anyone who wants his dog to be more than a house pet, is to advertise the dog as a pet, and either do not pass on the pedigree or write across the corner of it the reason for the dog being sold, in an attempt to prevent any unscrupulous individual breeding with the dog and perpetuating the problem. A good guide to how much to charge when selling a dog which is not making the grade as a gundog, but is otherwise a good dog, is to ask the current price of a new puppy, plus the cost of its inoculations. In this way a fair price is struck, giving the new owner a dog at a good price, which will have had quite a bit of its discipline training already completed, and therefore make it more desirable as a pet. At the same time this makes the pill that bit easier for you, the owner, to swallow, since at least you have recouped the basic costs of starting again.

Gun shyness and gun nervousness must never be confused. A dog which is gun nervous will get over it. In fact one of my own best bitches, when first introduced to shot was distinctly unhappy about the whole experience. So if your dog appears to be alarmed, frightened, or cautious, at the appearance of your starting pistol or gun, do not assume that it is gun shy. Rather apply a bit of intelligence and patience before deciding that it is beyond hope.

USE OF DUMMY LAUNCHER

As soon as your young dog is happy at the sound of your starting pistol, it is time to introduce the use of the dummy launcher. The best method of effecting the introduction of this is to sit the dog at a distance – twenty-five yards away from you. Let him see the starting pistol appearing, and fire it. The sight of it appearing, and the familiar shot will prepare him for the slightly louder bang of the launcher, plus the new sensation of a simultaneous obstacle flying through the air. Keeping the dog sat twenty-five yards from you, produce the dummy launcher. Push the dummy not more than half way down the spiggot, load it, and fire it, at a slight angle, above the parallel to the ground, and shoot it at a right angle to you and the dog. In this way he can see both you, and the launcher being fired, and will pick up the missile as it flies away.

By putting it half way down the spiggot you effectively reduce the power of the firing blank, and the dummy will only go a short distance, approximately thirty yards, the distance of a hand-thrown dummy. Do not be tempted to push the dummy all the way down the spiggot at this early stage, or you will launch the dummy much further (approximately ninety yards) than the dog has been used to working for you.

Watch the dog's reaction. It should be no more than one of slight surprise. Then retrieve the dummy yourself. Repeat the process. Retrieve it yourself again, then shoot it a third time, and this time, after the dummy has landed, wave the dog after the retrieve, with the command 'fetch' and give him the line to follow with your arm pointing towards the dummy. In this introduction to the dummy launcher always make sure, where possible, to throw the first few retrieves into short grass where the dog can see the retrieve. Take the retrieve from the dog,

Dummy launcher with black, white and ball dummies.

give him praise, and put the dummy launcher away. The lesson is finished for the day, and it is obviously always better when training a dog to finish on a high note.

Thereafter, in subsequent training periods, continue the use of the dummy launcher, gradually allowing the dog to come closer when you shoot, until eventually you are shooting the dummy launcher when he is sitting beside you. Remember always to command him to sit, in preparation for the dropping to shot lesson he will be taught fairly soon.

Progressively, over the next few weeks, push the dummy further down the spiggot, until the dog is being sent the full ninety yards the dummy is able to go. The distance you send your young dog on retrieves obviously depends on the sort of ground you are training him on. A young dog that has been used to being sent on retrieves some thirty yards distant is going to have to be gradually worked out further. There is no point in expecting an inexperienced young dog, irrespective of how good he appears to be at marking the line of a fallen dummy, to dash ninety yards through long bracken. That would be most unwise, and in the initial stages of the use of the dummy launcher restrict the long retrieves at maximum shot range, to short grass, where the dog is given the visual aid of seeing the dummy fall, whilst you yourself can keep the dog in sight at all times, so that you may correct or aid him if he starts to lose the place.

DISTANCE CONTROL WITH WHISTLE AND SIGNALS

One of the most necessary controls you must have over any gundog is to be able to stop the dog at distance, quickly and efficiently. There really is no reason why a dog should sit perfectly well on command ten yards from you, and not drop with equally crisp efficiency 150 yards away. Yet distance control is one of those thorny areas where many people find problems. The reasons for these problems are either a sloppiness in the training at close hand, with the owner not expecting nor getting crisp obedience, or the dogs have discovered what I call 'the influence barrier'. By that I mean the magical distance the dog has discovered, that once he has passed it he is out of your control.

How often have you heard people saying that their dog is perfect close at hand, but once it has reached a distance away, normally fifty yards or so, it ignores them. The reason is normally that the dog has misbehaved, perhaps spent more time sniffing a tasty scent at distance, and the owner has accepted this delay or lack of attention rather than getting after the dog immediately, bringing it to heel, and enforcing his will.

The other reason that people have difficulty at distance is because of the dog's lack of confidence when he is far away from you. The dog feels insecure and remote from the handler. All these problems of course can be avoided if the owner has diligently stuck to the correct training schedule when the dog was younger. If the dog.has been told to sit and remain whilst you walk long distances away before returning, if he has been taught to sit to the whistle when coming towards you, then he will sit automatically when the whistle sounds, and with a little practice, the sound of the whistle heard at distance and therefore quieter will mean the same as the loud whistle heard close at hand.

By now your dog will be sitting with hand, whistle and voice commands, and his reaction to any of these commands should be automatic; and whistle control at distance is really just a case of you stretching the distance between you and your dog, always striving to put greater distances between you.

Start off with the now familiar routine of leaving him sat, and walking a long distance away. Go out of sight and hide behind a tree or wall or any hiding place where he cannot see you but that you can peer around and keep your eye on him. Watch him closely, at the first sign of standing up, or curiosity, reappear and firmly blow the sit whistle and command him verbally to sit. Hopefully however, he will not be tempted to jump to his feet, but if he does you must realise that the dog is only anxious that you have gone off and left him, and the whole object of this exercise is to enforce on the dog the ability to remain where he is left until you return and collect him. At the same time you will be building in his mind a growing confidence in sitting alone, without you there as reassurance. This confidence building is vitally important, and you must always remember, when you reappear after a few minutes, to return to the dog nine times out of ten, so instilling in his mind the confidence that you will always return.

You can call him to you occasionally at distance with the recall signal of several small toots, to keep him sharp. However, do not be tempted to call him to you too often, otherwise you will quickly build in his mind the anticipation that he is about to be called to you, and you would soon discover his bottom off the ground and his whole being ready to spring after you, rather than the desired relaxed feeling of him sitting there, in the confident knowledge that there is no need to worry since you are sure to return.

The essence of distance control is, as I have said, continually stretching the distance between you and the dog as you give him a command. He will by now sit confidently fifty yards from you, come on the recall, and drop at the sound of your whistle when he is twenty-five yards from you. With care and systematic stretching of distance, you will soon find that you can blow the whistle commanding him to stop if you leave him at 100 yards, calling him in and stopping at say fifty yards.

There is however one danger area in all the recall commands, and it is one in which you must watch the individual dog for a sign of. That is the dog beginning to anticipate the sit command as he is running towards you. It can usually be seen quite easily. Having left your dog, let us say, 100 yards from you, and having got him used to you calling him in then dropping him half way, watch for hesitancy in the dog when he runs towards you. Is he running at a slower speed, as though waiting for the command to sit as you blow your whistle? If you see your dog behaving like this, give him a period of several days when you call him to you and do not command him to sit half way, before returning to the lesson. Always remember that in all dog training it is essential to ring the changes. Never do the same thing too often in succession, otherwise you will encourage your dog to start anticipating commands, which is very undesirable.

DISTANCE HAND SIGNALS

It is at distance that the sense of using the large, obvious and exaggerated hand signals that you have trained your dog with, will become apparent. Dogs are generally short-sighted, and a dog watching you from about 200 yards can only see your silhouette clearly. An arm held in front of you is lost in the silhouette, whereas an arm stuck straight in the air can be seen clearly. Equally, thigh patting, to bring the dog to you, should be a big movement; your straightened arm should come up at right angles to your body at shoulder height, and move up and down from the thigh.

RETRIEVING FROM WATER

Whilst most of your retrieving work will have been done on land, you will obviously have been building in a proportion of water retrieves and competence in water. Often this depends on proximity of water to your training areas, some trainers being forced to make a specific trip when water is not immediately available. But you will, wherever possible, have given the dog retrieves of the hand thrown dummy either from water or across water. The idea is purely to use the water as another location from which the dog must retrieve. After your dog has been introduced to the dummy launcher and is coming along with his land retrieves, you can start to incorporate the launcher into his normal water work, not so much to achieve greater range, since it is inappropriate to send a young dog on long swims out and back, and this must be carefully increased in direct proportion to his growing confidence and stamina. But the real benefit of the dummy launcher with water work comes from the combination of the shot that makes him sit as he looks about expectantly, and the dummy flying much faster than you can throw it, encouraging him to mark.

Care must be taken with water retrieves since it is the one element where you yourself cannot pick the retrieve, therefore, give him a restricted number of water retrieves in any training period, no more than one or two, and try always to follow water retrieving by a situation where the dog is required to sit whilst you pick two or three retrieves yourself from land.

A bold entry into water.

DROPPING TO SHOT

After your dog has become quite happy and relaxed at the report of your starting pistol, and has been introduced to the dummy launcher when he will have been told to sit prior to its use, you can start to teach him to drop to shot. This is a comparatively easily-taught lesson.

Sit the dog fifty yards from you, call him in to you, and when he is perhaps twenty-five yards away, throw your arm in the air as the visual command to sit and at the same time blow the whistle command to sit or give him the verbal command. Have the starting pistol in your left hand behind your back, and as you command him to sit, fire the pistol. He should automatically sit to the familiar command (whistle and arm) although almost certainly he will look around in surprise at the unexpected bang. Keep him in the sitting position for a few minutes before repeating the exercise. He will have sat to the familiar whistle, hand or voice command, and will soon over a few days, associate the pistol shot with the physical act of sitting and painlessly you will have taught him to drop to shot.

Dropping to shot. The young dog sent on a retrieve has stopped and sat to shot. Note the pistol held behind the handler.

More important is the time when you move to doing this exercise with the dog facing away from you. Cast him out when you go for a walk, and when he has his back to you blow the stop command on the whistle, whilst simultaneously firing a shot. If you have done the correct amount of groundwork with your whistle, he should sit automatically. After a few lessons you should be able to stop the use of other aids, and use the pistol shot only as a command to sit.

CROSSING OBSTACLES

The ability to cross obstacles, and the self-confidence to tackle walls, streams and fences, must be encouraged and brought out in all dogs. They have a natural ability to jump, but this ability can be refined and developed so that you instill in your dog confidence to launch himself at obstacles which would be daunting for an untrained dog. Personally, I am not happy with a dog that does not jump on command, but I would never put a dog over a strand fence. I have seen them not only pass a hind leg under the top wire, which can damage or break their leg, but I have also seen dogs badly injured by jumping barbed wire fences. I always teach a dog to go through such a fence when I open it.

STRAND FENCES

Sit your dog at your feet beside the fence. Open the fence, parting the wires with your left hand and foot, and throw a dummy through, encouraging the dog to go through after it. If necessary you can gently push the dog through the fence, whilst verbally encouraging him. Most dogs quickly learn this and it should be practised whenever possible in the training routine.

Low, tightly-strung sheep or rabbit fencing, where there is little chance of the dog getting caught in the fence, is the best place to teach a dog to jump. Cross the fence and walk on, encouraging the dog to follow you. He will either jump the fence and follow you, and thereafter require only practice, or more likely, he will run up and down the fence in confusion. Return to the fence, bring him to heel, let him know you are happy with him, produce your dummy, and throw it over the fence where he can see it, then lift him and drop him over the other side. I have never known a dog, once shown a couple of times what is expected of him, not take quite happily to this particular exercise. Remember that the command to cross a fence is 'over' and at all times from now on, whenever you put your dog over a fence, command it clearly with the simple word 'over'.

WALLS

Walls, since they have footholds, and are not as confusing to the dog as a fence which he can see through, are easier for him to jump. Therefore, a dummy thrown over a wall would normally encourage the dog to find its own way over. If your dog is reluctant to jump the wall, another technique is for you to sit on top of the wall and encourage the dog to follow you. He should normally then stand up against the wall, anxiously trying to get after you. All you do then is haul him up and let him drop over the other side. Or simply cross the wall, calling him over.

Cartridges.

When you first introduce your dog to a wall as an obstacle over which he must cross, it is obviously desirable to start with a low wall, throwing the dummy over, and commanding him to retrieve it, saying the word 'over' as he approaches the wall.

Then it should be a simple matter of progressing to higher walls which the dog must climb over.

STREAMS

Crossing a narrow stream can be strangely confusing for some young dogs. You cross it in one stride, and yet many young dogs will run up and down the bank in confusion, before apparently, in desperation, launching themselves across. Encourage your dog over, as before, and all should be well.

Once a young dog has learnt to jump it is a comparatively easy task to systematically increase the distance that you expect him to jump. There is obviously a limitation to how high a dog can jump over a fence with comfort and safety. Yet I have seen small labradors run straight towards an 8ft high rough stone wall, launch themselves up the wall, take a foothold, and pull themselves over. Even more surprising, I have seen them doing this carrying a goose in their mouths, and this only a few short months after they were introduced to the fact that they could jump at all. It all boils down to building self-confidence in the dog.

QUARTERING

All the other chapters in this book relate to the training of all gundogs. The only area where spaniels and pointers differ from retrievers is that spaniels are required to hunt, quarter, and drop to flush, and pointers are required to hunt, quarter, point, and drop to flush.

The art of quartering is purely a refined extension of your dog's natural abilities. It is you who shapes a nice uniform pattern for your dog, as it covers the ground in front of you, searching for any game that may be hidden, and either flushing, or pointing the game – and speed is the first consideration. How fast should your dog work? The eventual aim in any quartering dog is that it should cover its ground efficiently, miss nothing, and move at a speed which allows you to walk comfortably at your normal shooting pace. I am a great believer in the guide to game finding, given by a Seminole Indian to Howard Hill, the American bowhunter; 'walk little, look much'. Exactly the same motto applies to the modern rough shooter. You do not want a dog that covers ground like some canine missile, compelling you to bound along just to keep up or continually check the dog. To enjoy shooting correctly it is necessary that you walk slowly, which not only gives you time to take any shot that may arise, but allows you to take your time and enjoy the sport. So you must try to set a pattern in your dog that it works at the sort of speed you want to eventually achieve, neither too fast, nor too slow. Conversely, a dog which potters, trundling from one scent to another is every bit as undesirable as the opposite and speedy extreme.

The only difference between a spaniel quartering and that of an HPR is the range which the dog works. The spaniel should always work within shotgun range. I believe a spaniel should not quarter any further than twenty yards on either side of the gun, whereas a pointer should work ideally about fifty yards on either side of the gun.

There are two techniques used for quartering, one which involves the use of assistants and which I do not personally recommend since I believe the dog tends to divide his attention between the handler and the assistants. However, it is worthwhile mentioning here if you feel you would be happier working in this way. The handler, having first walked all game out of a large field, takes his dog to the side of the field where he is directed downwind. Then he sets off walking into the wind and casts the dog forward with a wave of his arm and the command, 'get on'. The two assistants, who are walking directly parallel to the handler, but the required distance of quarter (about twenty yards) to either side, start to alternate in calling the dog, as all three people walk slowly forward. In this fashion, all three proceed to walk slowly across the field with the dog running first this way and then that in front of the handler, who waves the dog on in the direction it is being called as it passes him. Whilst it is undeniable that this technique does work, not only does it put the handler in the position of having to rely on others, but I find the technique clumsy, and much prefer to train dogs to quarter with the handler alone.

The handler walks in a zig-zag course. As he starts to walk forward he gives the command 'get on' with a large and obvious wave of the arm. The dog will naturally run forward in front of the handler. When it reaches the required distance, the handler gives two or three peeps on the whistle, the recall signal, and immediately turns in the other direction. The dog will race after the handler, and as it passes him, with a big wave of the arm, he gives it the command to 'get on'. The dog will naturally run forward, whereupon the handler, on the dog reaching the required distance he wants it to turn on, gives the recall signal again, and turns away.

Handler demonstrating the big arm movement training a young springer to quarter (note whistle at the ready).

The dog quickly learns to enjoy this exercise, because he is being allowed to move unrestricted over the ground doing what his own instincts urge him to do – to run on testing the scents. As the dog becomes more proficient at running to one side and the other, the handler can progressively make the actual distance before turning less, until eventually the dog is running from side to side, with only the aid of the whistle to turn him, and the arm wave to send him on.

This quartering technique soon becomes imbedded into the dog's mind as a pattern, and after considerable practice he will naturally pace himself and turn before the handler has peeped the whistle. Work diligently with your dog at quartering, until you achieve a really nice, efficient technique. One method of helping to achieve this is to walk at right angles across the line of a ploughed field, casting your dog from one side to the other. Most dogs will then tend to quarter to each side of you, using the line of the furrows as a guide, and it certainly is a great aid in tidying up the crispness of the line your dog will quarter on.

A problem many inexperienced handlers find when teaching quartering is that the dog will not go out far enough, but don't be concerned. It is preferable for a young dog, when learning to quarter, to do shorter quartering which is controlled, rather than longer distance quartering, since once he gets into the field with wild game and once he experiences actual shooting days he will become confident in what he is required to do and will naturally pull out anyway.

As a good example, I have seen a pointer which quartered thirty yards on either side of the handler and seemed reluctant to stretch the range, to the point where the handler became quite frustrated. He asked me how he should go about getting further ranges. I advised him to do nothing, since it was preferable that the dog quartered as beautifully as he did at that time in his development. Over a subsequent shooting season, the dog learned, when working in a stubble field, to draw that bit further out, turning on the whistle. He needed only two reminders of where to turn before setting himself into the pattern of quartering that particular field. The same dog, when working a grouse moor, will pull even further. Therefore, if you have a dog which has a tendency to turn shorter than you ideally want, it is not normally a problem, since once they gain experience in the field they will naturally pull out that bit further.

Once your dog is quartering nicely, you must start judiciously dropping him on occasions, increasing your control of him. Watch until he is at full gallop then blow the stop whistle and make sure that he responds immediately. A dangerous area of behaviour, often overlooked until it is too late, is one of the quartering dog becoming so hyped-up on the quartering exercise that he forgets that he is working with you. However, do not overdo the exercise of stopping him when quartering too often, otherwise you may make him hesitant. It is desirable only to achieve a balance of control, rather than have the dog constantly expecting your command to drop.

Obviously the speed at which a dog will quarter in short grass is different from that which is required in cover, but your control of the dog and his understanding of turning to the whistle which keeps that invisible communication line between the two of you, must be absolutely unbroken before you move on to working him in more difficult sort of terrain.

When you first move to quartering him in cover, it is best to keep in either long grass or a root field or any form of vegetation where he will be slowed down and where he cannot see more than a few feet ahead. But it is essential when first moving a young dog into cover that it is not so long that you lose sight of him. Only after he has progressed to quartering in short cover and responding to the whistle should you move to longer cover; bracken, brambles, or similar thickets; it is vital you remember that he must be utterly reliable before you move him to the sort of situation where he is out of your sight. Otherwise you will not be able to see misdemeanors as they take place and take appropriate action.

A typical problem that the handler can face when he puts the dog to cover prematurely is that of the dog coming across a rabbit, and rather than dropping to flush or coming on point, he takes a few hesitant steps after the fleeing animal. Because he is out of your sight and you are unable to stop him, this is the moment when he first realises that perhaps he can chase undetected. I have on more than one occasion seen the results of premature introduction to cover, and once the bad habit is started it can be the very devil to stop. So it is much better to be on the safe side and avoid the temptation for a young dog until the lesson is thoroughly learnt.

POINTING

Some pointers will start to point from an early age. I have a young pointer puppy in my home, at the time of writing, who diligently points my wife's cat – under chairs, tables, or wherever the cat is currently trying to seek refuge – and the young dog is completely untrained. Conversely, other individuals may take some time before this natural instinct starts to develop – and pointing is a natural instinct. It is you, the trainer, who enhances, sculpts, shapes and develops what is already unborn. Don't concern yourself or panic if your pointer is over a year old and has not started to point. Concentrate on the other aspects of his training, whilst you wait for his pointing to appear.

Once you have noticed your dog is starting to point, then it is time to start giving him some help. It is advisable to go about this process with careful thought. Lay out the field where you intend to work the dog, giving consideration to cover, since you want to encourage your young dog to use its nose rather than its eyes. It is therefore desirable that the dog should always find with its nose rather than see the game. Long grass is ideal. Avoid training a young pointer in thick cover, such as bracken, where it may disappear from your sight. In all early stages of working with any young dog you must remember that when it is out of your sight it is able to commit small indiscretions of which you are unaware.

Having decided where you are going to work your dog then lay out either dizzied pigeons (*see* chapter 7, 'Dropping to flush'), or birds in small cages. Then, having cleared the game off the ground, work your dog, always at this early stage into the wind, towards where you know the bird to be placed. When using hidden game I strongly advise the use of a small stick marker so that you know exactly where the bird is.

When the young dog comes on point, approach it slowly and cautiously, giving it encouragement. Kneel beside it, gently stroke the dog and mould your hands to the dog's body. Smoothly run them from its head down its back and on to its flanks, and then right down to the tip of its tail. The idea of this gentle stroking is to calm and soothe the dog, keeping him in position and restraining him from any temptation to run forward. After a few minutes of this exercise, without flushing the bird, gently lead the dog away. Then, when he is well away from the bird, cast him on for a fresh point on your next hidden bird.

It is most unwise at the early stage of pointing to encourage a young dog to set up game, since all you are doing is encouraging him to run in and give chase. Your pup will of course have been taught to drop smartly to whistle by now, and therefore continue taking your dog out, giving him pointing experiences on your captive birds, always progressively lengthening the time you will keep the dog on point, styling him with your hands, soothing him with your voice. An added refinement, which is not necessary but adds a bit of style, is to gently lift one of your dog's front feet whenever it is pointing feathered game, and a hind leg if it is fur.

Once you reach the stage when your young dog is coming on point and rigidly holding it, then it is time to introduce him to the command of 'put up'. With your whistle ready to make him drop, encourage the dog forward, with the command 'put up', if necessary. If you are using a dizzied pigeon it may be necessary for you to gently slip your toe under the bird and flick it up. Immediately the bird springs, give the dog the command to sit. If the dog makes the slightest attempt to make a grab for the bird after being given the command to sit, immediately stop him with the command 'no'. With more fiery dogs it is sometimes necessary, when working the dog on to a point, to use a long check lead, so that you can gently restrain the dog from creeping forward. But try to restrict the use of the lead to the bare minimum and dispense with it at the earliest opportunity, since a dog quickly gets to recognise the difference between the restriction by the pressure of the lead on his neck, and freedom.

The most undesirable fault a pointer can possess is having an unreliable point as he gives in to the temptation of running in. Therefore a great emphasis should be made in keeping the dog rigidly on point. However, avoid allowing the dog to become so fixed in his point that he cannot be called off. Some pointers find it very difficult to break a point and only continual practice, over a period of weeks, can cure this minor problem as the dog grows to learn and understand what its trainer requires.

Once a young pointer can point keenly and then put the game out on the command 'put up' and neatly drop to flush, the handler can use captive game less and start to work the dog onto wild game. But you should not move to wild game until your dog is very confident in his pointing, flushing and dropping activities.

Whilst your dog has obviously been taught to quarter prior to pointing, it is at this stage that his quartering and pointing should be tightly merged into the one exercise, so that you can start to quarter him into side winds. It is ill-advised to make it any more difficult for your dog than is absolutely necessary. The wise handler should always use the wind to his best advantage by always working his dog into it until you reach the standard where your dog is quartering and coming on point beautifully every time.

You should not start to teach your dog to work a side wind until the whole technique of quartering into the wind and pointing game is firmly implanted in his mind. It does not normally take a dog long to realise that the most efficient way of finding game is with the wind blowing straight into his face. Once you have reached this stage with your dog you can start teaching him to work the wind, first from the side, and eventually with the wind coming from the handler's back. To work a side wind, send the dog forward in front of you and his function is to run back towards you, then out again, always using the wind. Equally, with the wind directly at the handler's back, the dog should be sent out well in front, in a straight line, some eighty to one-hundred yards with the 'go back' signal. He should then be stopped with the stop whistle and he should naturally look back at you for directions. He should then be given the visual signal of a wave to one side and the command 'get on'. If he has learned to work his wind correctly he will then quarter back towards you.

German shorthaired pointer on point in deep heather.

It must be emphasised however, that generally, the HPR breeds get better with experience as with all other aspects of gundog work. But in the use of the wind, the pointer becomes progressively more proficient as he educates his nose.

6. ONE YEAR TO EIGHTEEN MONTHS

By the time your young dog is a year old, it should be well on its way to being a gundog with a solid foundation of basic training. Over the next year you are going to train your dog in many interesting, different, and highly useful types of action which are all little more than variations of what you have already taught him. Because he has a good grounding in the basics it should be comparatively easy, much less frustrating and highly pleasurable for you to work with him.

Keep in mind, however, that this is not a race, and if your dog has not reached the standard that the book indicates there is no reason to become unduly concerned. All dogs are different, and just like children, some individuals have a capacity to learn faster and earlier than others. Others tend to be 'plodders' who develop later, and any book can only lay down guidelines as to what to expect. The only thing one must avoid is that if you have a particularly bright individual, do not race ahead.

It is vitally important that you are never tempted to try and advance a dog's training beyond the time guide, otherwise you could well get your dog, whilst he is still after all very young mentally, beyond the stage of true reliability. A young dog, for instance, should not be taken shooting or introduced to dead game before his training is well advanced. If you are fortunate enough to have a particularly bright individual, it is much more desirable to capitalise on the fact and concentrate on getting each individual lesson absolutely perfect. With all gundog training, there is a simple rule: if you find that your young dog is finding things difficult slow the training down. Conversely, if he is having no difficulty at all picking things up, then you can step up the training, but do not go too fast. Make the decision to suit the individual dog.

Up until now all the work you have done with your dog has been variations on the theme of obedience, constantly emphasising the control and communication between yourself and your dog. By now he should be a well-behaved, disciplined animal. He should by this time walk to heel, on or off lead, sit when you stop, remain where he is until told otherwise, run enthusiastically to retrieve both hand thrown and shot dummies, retrieve from water, sit to the sound of shot, whistle, hand and voice, either close at hand, or at distance, whether coming towards you or going away. He should generally be a pleasure to work with. It is over the next few months that you should increasingly begin to see the results of all the hard work you have done together.

DIRECTIONAL HAND SIGNALS

Start off with the dog close to you, about ten yards away. Throw a hand-thrown dummy to the left, keeping him in a sitting position. If, in all your preparatory work you have picked up the majority of dummies yourself, and always given sufficient period of time between the actual act of throwing the dummy and the command for the dog to retrieve it, then you should have no problems at this time. The dog should sit, watching the proceedings with interest, to see whether he is going to be allowed to pick the dummy. Giving him a big, obvious hand signal and with the command 'fetch' wave him towards the dummy. Take the retrieve, return the dog to his former position, and repeat the exercise, this time sending the dog on a retrieve to the right. Over the next few days, repeat these left and right retrieves.

Doing it this way, and taking time, normally results in this lesson being easily learnt and after a few days you can confidently progress to two dummies. Ideally you want to do these exercises using a fence or wall, as this assists the dog in running in straight lines. If you can practise making your dog run straight, either to the right or left (and later straight away from you) it will eventually make placing him on blind retrieves that bit easier.

With his back to a fence, stand about 10ft in front of your dog, and throw a dummy a short distance to the left, and another to the right against the fence. Hold your arm up in the

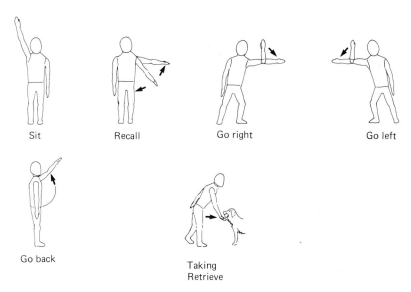

Sit   Recall   Go right   Go left

Go back

Taking
Retrieve

Hand signals.

sitting position, and let the dog register that there are two dummies. Dogs will always naturally want to go for the last dummy thrown. This is the most immediate in the dog's mind and is obviously the one he would much prefer to pick, so, in keeping with the whole theory of your mind always controlling the dog's, direct him on to the first dummy thrown with the command 'fetch'. Be prepared, if he breaks towards the other dummy, to quickly blow the stop whistle and drop him, waving him on to the one you wish him to retrieve.

If the dog, in his excitement, goes towards the other dummy and doesn't stop on the whistle, take the retrieve as though nothing had happened. When you repeat the exercise stand much closer to him so that you can physically stop him if necessary.

Return the dog to the sitting position, then wave him to retrieve the other dummy. Vary this particular exercise, increasing the distance between yourself and the dog whilst simultaneously increasing the distance of the retrieves, and after a couple of weeks you should have reached the stage where you can throw a dummy well to the left and right, walk a good fifty yards out into the field away from the dog, and then on the visual signal combined with the 'fetch' command, direct him to whichever dummy you want.

A variation on the direction of left and right is that of going straight away from you. This is best done, if possible, on a path during a normal walk with your dog. Take a dummy out, let the dog see it, then throw it a few yards back down the path. Walk on with your dog at heel for a short distance (about ten yards) make him sit, then standing in front of him, wave your arm out straight above your head with the command 'go back'. Your dog will show one of two reactions. He will either turn and immediately run back for the dummy, or cast about unsure of what is wanted. If he casts about obviously having forgotten about the dummy, then you have simply walked too far and let too much time pass between throwing the dummy and sending him back.

Collect the dummy yourself and repeat the exercise, this time shortening the distance you walk before sending him back. The encouraging sound of your voice as you send him is normally enough to get him dashing back for the dummy, and once he has had a few opportunities to go back he will quickly pick up this new command.

Now repeat the exercise against the fence. Sit him beside the fence, facing you. Throw the dummy over his head, walk away a few yards, then send him back, with your arm straight above your head and the command 'go back'. Practice, a little but often, is the secret. One or two retrieves during every training session should be enough. Progressively move yourself further from the dog and the retrieves further away and you will soon find that you can stand 100 yards away from your dog and direct him to the left, right, or straight away from you.

ADVANCED DUMMY RETRIEVING

When a dog has reached a level of confidence in himself and his surroundings, and is happily retrieving dummies, either thrown or shot from a launcher, you can progressively start to move him through a whole series of advanced dummy retrieving exercises. His retrieving to date will have been a mixture of dummies, (fur and feather) thrown and shot, and by now he will be retrieving from both water and light cover. The term 'advanced dummy retrieving' means quite literally that you can make the retrieves progressively more difficult as you strive to recreate the ever differing retrieves and obstacles which the dog must face to carry out the task of retrieving.

Remember that all your training is aimed at producing the sort of gundog you can be proud of; the sort of dog that you can take to a shoot, whether it is a formal driven bird or a day's rough shooting with a friend, and one that you should confidently be able to send on any retrieve that may present itself.

You should slowly start to make the whole business of re-trieving more difficult. Use your imagination to utilise whatever natural configuration the ground you use for training has. If there are no fences with sheep or rabbit netting on them in your area for instance, then it makes sense to build a fenced-in square – if you can borrow sufficient net fencing, posts and a piece of ground. Into this square you can throw your dummies so that at least you can send your dog on a retrieve involving a fence that needs jumping. Whatever you do you must avoid compla-cency or lack of imagination.

Steadiness control in company. Here the handler will throw the dummy and allow one dog to retrieve. The other two are compelled to observe and maintain position.

A good example of poor gundog training was once shown to me by a good friend who brought his five-year-old labrador bitch with him when he visited me. This was a dog which was excellent in all forms of retrieving, with one exception. To my absolute astonishment, when walking around the loch near my home, I discovered that the dog had never actually been swimming. My friend explained to me that in the area of England where he lived there were no waterways beyond the odd ditch, and he had never taken the trouble to take his dog to water.

By this time in his training, your dog will obviously have grasped firmly the whole idea of retrieving, and he will look forward to his training outings, so start making him work that bit harder.

Sit the dog in front of you, shoot the dummy over his head so that it goes directly behind him, then leaving him sat, walk directly away from him in the opposite direction to where you have left the dummy. Call him to you by hand or whistle and when he is half way stop him on the whistle, and giving him the 'go back' signal with hand and voice, send him back for the dummy. This distance of 'go back' can be worked with him quite easily up to at least 200 yards.

A variation of the same exercise, which requires a large field, is to sit the dog in the middle of the field, shoot a dummy on either side of him, then walk about 100 yards away. After a short wait send the dog on the retrieve. Immediately blow the stop whistle. Once he has sat, wave him to retrieve the other dummy. Take the retrieve, make him sit and send him to pick the dummy still in the field. There are many other variations. Shoot a dummy into cover where the dog can only see the line of its fall, but not the exact location, then send him out on a retrieve. Shoot a dummy over a wall, or over water, into cover where it cannot be seen, and send the dog on a retreive. Shoot three dummies in three different directions, one after the other, and then send the dog to pick two of them retrieving the third yourself. Continually strive to create new, challenging retrieves for your dog.

Advanced dummy retrieving is designed to prepare the dog for the next and much more difficult retrieving training, that of blind retrieving. So, the more preparation and the more you can smooth the way through your dog's education by a constant and steady increase in the difficulty and complexity of the tasks you put him to, the easier it will be for the dog to continue his development.

By this stage in his training, if you always stretch the distances you send the dog for a retrieve, and the time you keep him waiting between shooting the dummy and sending him for it, you will have extended his capacity to mark and remember. The 'go back' signal is a perfect example of quite how surprising some dogs' memories can be, and if it is done with a gradual increase in time and distance, your dog's mental capacity can be improved and developed.

A good example, though by no means rare or unusual, is a young dog which, at the time of writing, I am in the middle of training. A few months ago, if I dropped a dummy in sight of him and walked on with him at heel for much more than fifty yards, and waited too long (even the time it took me to fill and light my pipe) he would already have forgotten. Yet now, walking around the loch near my home, I can stop him, make him sit, throw a dummy down, then walk on with him at heel several hundred yards before telling him to sit. Standing in front of him you can see the anticipation in his face as he waits for the command to go back, which he does with unerring accuracy.

Yet even with a bright dog, small obstacles that seem simple to us can quite surprisingly upset the canine mind. For instance, if you throw a dummy down and take the dog away with you on the by now familiar walking to heel, then cross a high wall and walk on another fifty yards prior to sending him back, you will often find that the dog will run quickly back to the wall, and then cast up and down the wall as though he has forgotten where the retrieve lies. The answer is to give him more practice at shorter distances until he is confident about crossing anything in his path.

Advanced retrieving is largely dependent upon the facilities that you have, whether it be a public park, farmland, woodland, or seashore. Utilise cover and distance. Don't be afraid to send a dog on a retrieve, to stop it half-way and either move it to another retrieve or give him the recall. Confidently remain in control of your dog and you will find these lessons easily learnt.

BLIND RETRIEVES

So far, all retrieving training and whistle-control work has been to prepare your dog for a long blind retrieve where he has no idea where the game is. Every gundog owner dreams of being at a shoot when he is asked to send his dog on some long and distant retrieve where a bird has been reported to have fallen and to the astonishment and delight of the watching guns he can direct his dog, with a minimum of fuss, into the area of the fallen bird. Yet this ability is comparatively easily achieved if your dog's training has been consistently progressive, from puppyhood discipline to advanced dummy retrieving at distance.

If your dog has become used to working far from you, yet still being responsive to the whistle and is therefore at all times under control, it is time to introduce him to blind retrieves. Like all other forms of gundog training, it is always best to start off making things easy by working at close range. When you go to your training ground, whether you walk or drive,

This photograph perfectly demonstrates the handler intelligently using the ground for training, having thrown the dummy on to the bank above the tree stump on the left, the young dog is required to mark across a gulf, then run downhill over a stream and uphill to find the retrieve, with the added advantage of returning up a steep slope, which builds back and thigh muscles.

leave your dog sitting at the edge of the field and walk off any game that might be there. As you are doing this surreptitiously drop a dummy in some long grass where the dog cannot see you drop it and return to the dog. Walk him into the wind, sit him about twenty yards from where you know the dummy lies upwind of him, step back from him and give him the signal to fetch, giving him the line. If there is any reluctancy in him, remember that up until now he will have been used to a dummy being thrown or shot, encourage him on with additional commands to fetch, using the arm waving technique to show him the line. As he runs forward towards the area of the dummy, give him the by now familiar command 'steady' and you will find that with the aid of the scent of the dummy in his nose, he should quickly find it.

As soon as he picks it encourage him back, and make a fuss of him. Continue this particular exercise over several training outings until you are sure that he is quite confident in going out for this simple blind retrieve, either to left or to right, according to your signal. But try at all times to use the wind to aid your dog in finding the dummy during these early stages.

The next progressive step is to go back to your training area. Sitting your dog and walking off the game as before, drop your hidden dummy, go back and collect your dog and take him out onto the field, sitting him in position as though you were going to send him for the hidden dummy. Then produce your other dummy and throw it clearly were he can see it, in the opposite direction from where the hidden one lies. Then after a short wait, send him for the hidden dummy. Obviously, his temptation is to go for the one he saw falling. Do not allow this, and wave him to the other one. When he picks it, make a fuss of him, and then leaving him sat, walk to the other dummy and let him see that you are retrieving it. The whole idea of these early blind retrieving exercises is to place in your dog's mind the confident knowledge that when you wave him in a particular direction, he will find a retrieve.

As your blind retrieving training progresses, you will know how fast to move your young dog. Go to a training area and walk off the game. Put out several retrieves, throwing them into cover, over streams or walls, or wherever you can hide them. Then get the dog and walk slowly around the circuit where you know the dummies are secreted. As you approach each hidden dummy, fire your starting pistol, giving the dog the drop-to-shot command. Then carefully wave it out on a blind retrieve with the fetch command, giving encouragement when the dog returns with the dummy. It is permissible by this time in the dog's training to give it up to half a dozen blind retrieves in these outings. However, keep your eye on your dog and watch him carefully. If he is becoming too fired up or over-exuberant on these retrieves, drop the number you give him back to two or three in each training session.

As your dog's competence on blind retrieves progresses, a nice variation to introduce him to is to retrieve tennis balls. Introduce him to the tennis ball as an object you want retrieved. To aid him in scenting, rub it either through your hair, or in the armpit of your shirt. What you are doing is giving it a pungent smell, which his keener nose will be able to pick up. Once he understands that the tennis ball is for retrieving then you can walk a circuit prior to taking him out and knock balls into cover, bracken, brambles etc. with a tennis racket. Use them for blind retrieves when you go back to get the dog.

The tennis ball technique is purely a variation of the shot dummy. Most people can lay their hands on an old tennis racket, and half a dozen balls are a great deal cheaper than half a dozen launcher dummies. Again, imagination is the watchword with blind retrieves. Hide them behind walls, throw them over streams, then carefully and quietly work your dog on to the dummy by giving him the hand signals that he is now familiar with: go back, left, right, and call 'steady' as he nears the area you wish him to search.

An excellent technique to employ when working on blind retrieves is to shoot a dummy well to the right and in front of you. Then send the dog out for it on a sighted retrieve. As he nears the area, blow the stop whistle and allow him to collect himself as he sits and watches you, then wave him away to the left, away from the dummy that he has seen fall, and work him onto a hidden blind retrieve that you have previously secreted. A variation is to do this across water.

As in all other training exercises, not only does practice make perfect, but by continually increasing the complexity of task and distances which you send him and expect him to work, you will be highly rewarded as you see him developing into the finished gundog.

ADVANCED WATER WORK

Up to this point your dog will have been gaining experience swimming in whatever water you have handy, doing small retrieves in the natural course of his training. As your dog's proficiency, expertise and self-confidence in the water increases, you can move to more advanced water work. However, make sure that you do not lose sight of the fact that your young dog is an athlete and he must be physically trained and be ready for any form of advanced water training. If a dog is tired or fatigued in the field, you often do not see it because he can slow down or stop, and since few shooting activities call for a dog to move constantly without being given the chance to rest, then you are less likely to see your dog flagging until he becomes physically very tired indeed. Certainly at the end of the day, your dog may be so tired that he flops down in the back of the car and soundly goes to sleep. But during the day when he will have taken short pauses to recoup his energy, or at least paced himself to conserve energy, if you have noticed it at all you will have accepted it for what it is – him taking a rest.

However, a dog swimming in water has no such recourse to take a rest. Unlike a human who can roll on his back and float if he is fatigued, a dog must keep swimming or quickly get into difficulties. From the moment his body becomes buoyant as he leaves the shore, until his feet touch the shore on his return, he is constantly active. Also, there is the cold. Water draws heat twenty times faster than air and consequently you have a situation where the dog, dependent on its physical abilities and condition, has obviously got limited time in which it is safe for him to be in water. And, of course unlike a human, a dog has no way of knowing when he must turn back or that he must keep sufficient energy in reserve to swim safely back to shore.

A dog, with a bird swimming in front of him, could quite easily swim on after the bird, his determination to get it putting himself in such a position that when he turns, exhausted, he does not have sufficient stamina left to reach safety. Even if he does, he may have seriously damaged his cardio-vascular system. Therefore, if there is the slightest chance of you working your dog in water, you must make considerable efforts to get him into the right condition, while at the same time working on his obedience in water, so that he can not only take directions, but will answer immediately if given the recall.

A dog's response to hand signal direction and whistle must be highly developed on land before you can safely and confidently start making him change direction in water. On land for example, you will by now be able to throw or shoot a dummy to either side of him, or straight over his head, keep him in a sitting position and give him the command to either go back or to retrieve left or right. You always have the insurance policy that if the dog goes in the wrong direction you can stop him and re-direct him. Also, part of the training for obedience to hand signals on land is to send him to one side on a retrieve, and half way to it, stop him and redirect him. Once the dog has reached this stage in his land work, then you can start giving him the same commands in water, with a dummy shot out to the left or right and giving him the command to fetch. As he sets off in one direction, you blow the stop whistle. Obviously the dog cannot sit in water, but he will, and should, respond to the whistle by slowing down, or looking back at you. Then you wave him to the other dummy. If you have diligently worked on his hand signals on land retrieves, it takes a very short time before the dog learns the technique of treading water, or swimming in a half-circle, watching you when given the stop whistle. Work on your hand signals in water at short distances, only progressing to longer retrieves as the dog becomes more expert.

For hidden water retrieves you will find the real benefit of having given him a line direction. The technique in water is exactly the same as on land. You will previously have thrown a dummy into a reed bed, where it cannot float or drift away. Then, returning with your dog to the bank where you know the retrieve is, line him up in the direction you want him to swim, and give him the command to fetch. The first couple of times he does this in the water, he will most likely jump in, swim out, and then look back at you for direction. Do not give him directions that are too distant but make it easy for him to find the hidden retrieve. Then, as you progress in his water work, you will be able to work him at ever increasing distances.

One of the greatest problems faced by many gundog owners with water work is getting a dog to cross a river, canal, or waterway, exit on the other side, and go up over the bank, working on a blind retrieve. Most dogs seem either reluctant or unsure of what the handler wants, and the only way to achieve success is to utilise water wherever possible as only part of the obstacle course between him and the retrieve. Once the dog is working well on land to hand signals, going left, right, or back the distances that you introduce him to work after crossing water should be reduced.

Water brings another element or obstacle into the dog's mind, and if your dog is at the stage of working 100 or 200 yard retrieves on land, his cross water retrieving at that time should not be expected to be more than 50% of his land distance. Make it easy for your dog. Remember that there is nothing more rewarding for you or your dog than the successful retrieve after a hunt, so it is best to avoid confusing the dog.

If you throw or shoot a dummy to the other side of a river where a dog can see it, send him across the water with the command 'fetch' and give him the line. As soon as he reaches the other bank, stop him, make him sit, then give him the hand signal and the command to fetch again. As he grows used to taking the by now familiar hand directions after he has crossed water, you should have little difficulty progressing him on to hidden retrieves.

There is really no difference between sending your dog on a long retrieve across a field, stopping it on the whistle, and directing it on to a hidden dummy, and sending one first of all across a river, and then on a long retrieve. The only difference in technique is that you advance the land retrieves ahead of your progression across water retrieves.

If every time they enter water they bring out a retrieve, most dogs think that it is in the water that the retrieve is to be found. They show a marked reluctance to exit water, go up the opposite bank, over, and out of sight, preferring to cast up and down the opposite bank. Even well-trained dogs in this situation can appear oblivious to the handler's commands. But this will not be the case if you give the water no more significance than any other obstacle such as a wall, and give the dog plenty of experience of crossing the water and then taking hand signals. Always remember to stop the dog on top of the other bank, just before he goes out of sight, since this may be your last opportunity to give him a hand signal before he is working out of your sight.

A good example of this was a dog belonging to a man I was once shooting with. The dog had been well trained and was excellent, but had never really had any experience of crossing water and leaving it to get the retrieve. My companion shot a duck which landed neatly on the middle of a little island, about fifty yards from the bank of the small loch where we were shooting. It was obvious the bird had fallen dead and should have been relatively simple to retrieve. The dog had not seen where the bird landed, and when it was sent out on the retrieve took the line beautifully. He swam out with great enthusiasm, working the air and craning his neck to look for the bird he could not smell. The owner of the dog directed it nicely and eventually the dog actually waded into the shallow of the island, looking back at the owner for directions. But no matter how often he told it to go back, the dog was obviously convinced the bird was in the water and was reluctant to leave it. In fact, the dog never did pick the bird, and had to be recalled.

I had a young dog with me who was a great deal less experienced, but had had the benefit of more distance direction, and of crossing water on retrieves. Only a small part of its water retrieves ever having been actually in the water. When the dog was recalled I sent my young dog across, and directed it on to the edge of the island where I blew the stop whistle, commanding the dog to sit. It looked back at me expectantly, and I gave it the straight go back signal. As it disappeared into the vegetation I gave it the steady command to indicate that it was near the retrieve. The dog quickly reappeared with the duck and came straight back. The young dog was not as experienced as the older dog but had had the benefit of being directed across water, with obviously satisfactory results.

DOUBLE RETRIEVES

Possibly the most frustrating thing that can happen when you are shooting is for a dog on its way back with a retrieve to break the line and go for another bird. Now whilst this is a relatively simple thing to avoid on land, where again you can command your dog to sit, it is slightly more difficult in water. But if you have prepared the dog thoroughly with his hand signals and if he has learned the word 'no', then you should encounter few difficulties when you advance him to double retrieves.

Have two dummies ready to hand throw. Take your dog to

the water's edge, give it the command to sit, and throw a seen dummy far out into the water. Line the dog up and send it on the retrieve. When the dog is half way back to you, throw the second dummy over its head. If the dog hesitates or makes the slightest movement to turn after the second dummy, immediately and sharply say 'no' and encourage the dog to come back to you. When it has exited the water, and you have taken the retrieve it is permissible, after a short delay, to send the dog on a second retrieve.

It is also of great advantage if you have access to an older well-trained dog at this stage. After you have taken the first retrieve from the young dog and told it to sit, send the other dog for the second retrieve, keeping the young dog in a sitting position, observing throughout, whilst the older dog gets the retrieve, brings it back, and hands it over. Once the young dog has the idea that it must ignore the other dog, then you can progress to sending the older dog on the second retrieve whilst the young dog is still returning.

Do not however do this initial double retrieve by sending the older dog too close to the younger dog – keep the retrieve to one side. As the younger dog gains expertise it will soon become possible to throw the dummy straight over the returning dog's head and send the second dog on a retrieve, compelling both dogs to swim past each other within a few feet and yet ignoring each other.

BRINGING OUT THE GUN

In all training exercises, as your puppy grows to a fully-trained young dog, it is essential to review the different training techniques which will eventually build into a simulated day's shooting. So in all training trips out of doors you should run over everything you have previously taught your dog.

Obviously, when it comes to the introduction of you carrying the gun, the dog is going to see another aspect of his work. You are going to look different. Instead of the familiar picture of you with your game bag, dummies, dummy launcher, starting pistol, lead, you are now going to be carrying an unfamiliar object. So again approach it sensibly. Set out on your training schedule, running over everything the dog has done to date. Walk him at heel, walk in a zig-zag course varying the speed and making sure that he drops quietly when you stop. Leave him sitting, walk away and return to him. Exactly as you introduced your dog to the sound of the starting pistol, use an assistant who should walk fifty yards away and fire his gun in the air. Watch the dog for any sign of alarm. If he is frightened, then put off the exercise for another day. Move the gun ten yards closer each time it is fired until it can be fired beside the dog. It is unusual that a dog which has already become used to the shot of a starting pistol and dummy launcher, will show any undue alarm at the fresh bang and he should quickly take it in his stride. The reason for first firing the gun that bit further away is purely caution. The shotgun will make a louder, different sound to the starting pistol. It may seem at this stage in the dog's training that I am being over cautious, but I am a great believer in taking no chances whatsoever when introducing a young dog to any new experience.

From now on, take your gun with you whenever possible. You are, after all, now working towards a simulated day's shooting, and a typical training period should contain all the constituent parts of his training to date. But each exercise should be a separate command and task to be performed, rather than them all running together too quickly. Use the shotgun frequently instead of the starting pistol in your dropping to shot lessons.

INTRODUCTION TO DEAD GAME

It is imperative that no gundog should ever be introduced to game as an object to be retrieved, until all his training is largely complete. Up until now all the work you will have done with him will have been under the controlled conditions of retrieving dummies. The fur and feather covering that you have fitted is purely to get him used to the texture in his mouth, and he must not, up until this stage, have been introduced to animals, alive or dead. He must think they have nothing to do with him, until you come to introduce him to dead game. The reason for this is that your dog must be under your control at all times, be well-mannered and versed in all forms of retrieving, prior to the excitement that strong smells and dead animals encourage. A dog that has been introduced to the delights of carrying dead animals and has had his hunting instincts enhanced is going to find it a great deal more difficult when first brought to the rabbit pen, and expected not to chase, if he has already experienced carrying game in his mouth. Therefore, the introduction to game is reserved until near the end of his training.

The best type of dead game to introduce your dog to is the smaller, more easily-carried specimens – partridges or rabbits, eventually moving on to pheasants and ducks. Do not be tempted, no matter how strong and large a beast your dog is, to ask him to retrieve hares, unless they are very small, or geese for that matter, until he has become well experienced in carrying game. Not only do the large creatures such as hares and geese present a young dog with difficulties because of their weight, but also you can easily find that in order to give himself better grip on heavier objects he must squeeze tighter and this can encourage a hard mouth. So continue with the principle we have so far employed throughout the dog's training: make things as easy as possible whenever introducing your dog to a new experience.

If you can procure rabbits which are snared, so much the better, since it is not desirable, whatever you are going to use, that it should have blood on it. If you are using shot game it is wise to sponge off any blood to avoid the dog getting it in his mouth. If he does it may encourage him either to stop and lick the wound or make him hesitant to pick it up while he stops and has a good sniff. Ideally, when introducing your young dog to his first dead game, you are best to use rabbits which have not been paunched, and for convenience sake, it is a simple matter to have put a small store of these in the deep freeze. Take it out of the freezer the night before. If you are using fresh game, let it go cold before you use it.

The procedure is exactly the same as when you first introduce him to the furred or feathered dummy in place of the canvas one. Take him out to the training ground, throw him a retrieve and send him for it. Take it from him and immediately throw a dead rabbit, and send him after that. As soon as he nears the rabbit, give him much encouragement, calling him back. Take the retrieve gently from his mouth with the word 'dead', give him much praise and immediately put the rabbit away in your game bag out of sight. If he has a sniff at the rabbit before picking it, don't be surprised, but do encourage him on, if necessary running away from him. Occasionally it happens that a dog may be reluctant to pick game. Don't be concerned about this, try it again, and if he continues to refuse, put it away and try it again another day, slotting the retrieves into the beginning of his training schedule when you are first out and when he will be fresh and exuberant.

I do not recommend the continuous use of the same dead specimen, and I much prefer to use one animal per retrieve, since the dog will have put saliva on the rabbit. But if you are short of game, it is permissible to re-use it. Try, however, to restrict yourself to a maximum of three retrieves with the same specimen.

Once the dog has been introduced to retrieving game, then you can start to vary the retrieves, using as wide a variety of specimens as you have available. One bird I would not advise you to use with any young dog is the wood-pigeon. They have particularly dirty, loose feathers, and there is nothing as discouraging for a dog as running out full of enthusiasm, bringing you a retrieve, and then standing with a mouthful of dry feathers which he has difficulty spitting out.

As you start to use larger specimens you may find, if you have a small dog that some species require a little preparation, until he gets used to picking and balancing game. Cock pheasants are easier for a small dog if the tail feathers are pulled out. This will stop him treading on them as he is running back to you. Equally, it is not wise, as I have said, to put a young dog to retrieve geese, since with their long trailing neck and wings all too often a young dog ends up standing on them and tripping over. The whole idea is to make things easy for your dog. Let him become perfectly happy, relaxed and confident in his retrieves with dead game, before you gradually give him heavier specimens.

TAKING A LINE

Whilst all gundogs have a natural ability to follow a scent line, this natural ability can be enhanced, nurtured and developed. The advantages of being able to follow a line are obvious, the most immediate being that up until now retrieves the dog has found have been from a single scent source - where the dummy has lain after it has fallen. Now, with the aid of a dead rabbit, we are going to develop the use of his nose and encourage him to work out scents.

Whilst it is entirely permissible to use a piece of rabbit skin, I personally find that it is best to use the whole dead rabbit. The butt of a salmon rod or even a broom shaft with a couple of eyelets with a large fishing reel fitted to it, are ideal for this purpose. Tie the end of your fishing line to a rabbit's back leg. You are going to drag it backwards against the lie of the fur, to give a marginally stronger scent.

Go to your training area. Walk, about thirty yards from the area of long grass where you intend to throw the rabbit, throw it out and then walk off, paying the line out as you go. After you have walked about thirty yards, walk across at right angles to the line you have taken and reel the rabbit in. It is imperative that you lay the rabbit line into the wind. Untie the rabbit and leave it in long grass. You do not drag the rabbit behind you because then your scent would intermingle with the rabbit's on the line. It is much better to give the exercise that little bit of extra effort and lay a separate line of rabbit scent for your dog to follow.

Get your dog from the car or house, and then work him into the wind. As he nears where you know the line begins, he should start to show the signs indicating that he is on to a scent – the nose closer to the ground, the tail wagging and general signs of excitement. Fire a shot, either from your starting pistol, or your shotgun if you have it with you, which should compel the dog to drop. Give him a short time sitting, then give him the command to fetch and the line to follow. As he nears where you know the game to be encourage him by repeating 'steady' once or twice. Then when he picks the retrieve and brings it in, give him praise, take the retrieve, put it in your game bag, and continue on.

7. EIGHTEEN MONTHS TO TWO YEARS

By this stage in your dog's education he will have progressed almost to the point of being fully trained, and as far as his general obedience, work with directional signals, retrieving of dummies and cold game are concerned, he should be spot on. The only game that he has seen until now will have been dead. It is however time to introduce him to the ultimate temptation – live game.

Let me emphasise that this is one particular aspect of your dog's training that can in no way be either short-circuited or otherwise got round. He must be absolutely reliable in all aspects of live game if you are going to avoid the ultimate nightmare of all gundog owners, the crime of running in. There is nothing more demoralising to any field sportsman than a dog which gives chase. Some of the most potentially superb dogs I have seen have been rendered completely useless by the fact that as soon as live game appears in front of them they have a tendency to take off. It cannot be tolerated, it must never be allowed to happen, and if correctly approached, should never happen.

Your dog should by now be 100% reliable to the stop whistle and sitting on command. More importantly, you will by now have built a communicative understanding between your dog and yourself. He should be well able to recognise your moods and intentions and should understand the inflections of your voice. You in turn should be experienced at reading your dog, observing the signs that they all give as individuals when they are getting excited. But most important, this communications bridge, the bond which good gundogs and their handlers must have, should be well established.

If you have worked diligently with your dog, if you have

followed each stage in this book and made sure that each addition to his training schedule has been thoroughly and completely learnt, then when you introduce him to live game you should have such an excellent control and communications line between you that the rabbit pen will give few problems.

THE RABBIT PEN (Dropping to Flush)

It is desirable that gundogs should drop to flush. I personally prefer them to sit, rather than just stand, when game is flushed, since the action of sitting (placing their bottoms on the ground) is to my mind more positive than a dog which just stops. In training a dog to drop to flush, the use of the rabbit pen is invaluable.

Rabbit in rabbit pen.

If you can construct a rabbit pen so much the better. The size is governed by the amount of ground you have available, and how much you can afford to spend. If, on the other hand, these facilities are impossible for you, then contact your nearest professional gundog trainer and ask him if you can have access to his pen, explaining the reason why you need it. Most gundog trainers would be happy to encourage you. If there are no professional trainers with rabbit pens in your area, then approach a keeper on a nearby estate, and ask him if you can use one of his release pens when it is not in use. Whatever type of pen you use, it is essential that you have in it half a dozen rabbits, and perhaps even one or two pheasants, with their primary wing feathers pruned to stop them flying. Under these controlled conditions, where you know you can flush a rabbit, you will find it that bit easier than just making do with working your dog in the open, in the hope that you can blow your whistle simultaneously to flushing a rabbit.

Take your dog on the lead into the rabbit pen, and walk it at heel around the pen, until the dog sees a rabbit. Immediately the dog spots the rabbit command it to sit. Repeating the word 'sit' take the lead off and walk around the pen, flushing the rabbit. Keep your eye on your dog, and if there is the slightest temptation in him to chase, command him to sit. If by any chance he chases a rabbit, blow your stop whistle, get after him, grab him and roughly drag him back to where he had originally been placed. Give him a shake, and again command him to sit. Then repeat the process of walking up the rabbits.

The whole idea of this exercise is to make the dog quite used to sitting, whilst all these temptations hop about within his sight. After a few lessons, once it is obvious the dog has the idea that it must not chase, when you next go into the rabbit pen, walk the dog around. In the case of a spaniel or pointer you can cast it out, but watch the dog. The instant a rabbit bolts in front of it, blow the stop whistle, commanding it to sit. Allow the dog to sit, watching the game disappear, then go to the dog and make a fuss of it. Let it know you are well pleased, then continue the exercise, giving it two more flushes.

Once your dog has experienced many trips to the rabbit pen over several weeks, he should be absolutely steady to game. Add in the variation of giving him a short retrieve with the hand-thrown dummy through the rabbit pen. Be particularly careful when you first introduce him to a retrieve in the pen that he doesn't suddenly succumb to the temptation, now that he is on his feet and moving, of having a quick burst after something he may flush. So be ready with your stop whistle. However, if you have meticulously worked at keeping him

The ideal addition to the rabbit pen, which can of course be eventually released.

steady in the pen over the last few weeks this should not arise.

Obviously, the rabbit pen has its limitations. Eventually the dog becomes familiar with the expected regime, when he is taken into the pen, and it is, after all, just to prepare him for the experience of flushing game in the field. The pen is invaluable throughout a dog's life. I am a real believer in occasional refresher courses before the beginning of any shooting season. They sharpen a dog up and remind him that game is not for chasing.

At this stage in his training it is time to take him out of the rabbit pen and let him experience wild game that he is not prepared for. The best technique is to go to an area where you know you will find rabbits and the best time to do this is early in the morning. Rabbits sit tighter early in the morning. Later in the day they are more likely to bolt much sooner.

Working your dog into the wind, towards where you would expect a rabbit to sit, have your stop whistle ready, and the instant they flush, blow the whistle. In these early excursions in the field don't wait to see if he sits without the aid of the whistle but use the extra small insurance policy of this aid commanding him to sit, while the rabbit bolts. You can, after several days, delay the use of the whistle to see if he sits, but have it ready to refresh his memory if he doesn't sit immediately. If there is the slightest temptation to chase, the best course of action is to return to the rabbit pen and give him further tuition.

An alternative to the use of rabbits, and one which I am keen on using is that of dizzied, or captive pigeons. The advantage of using a pigeon is that the dog cannot possibly chase it since the bird quite literally flies away. Contact your nearest pigeon fancier and approach him, on bended knee, for the occasional loan of one of his least valuable birds. Explain to him that the

Steadiness in the game pen demonstrated by a young labrador with three cock pheasants.

bird will come to no harm, and obviously assure him that if it doesn't return you will happily reimburse him for the loss of the bird.

The dizzied pigeon technique is relatively simple to employ.

Hold the bird gently in both hands, and carefully push its head under one wing. Then holding it upside down (see illustration) move it gently in a circular motion for a minute. The bird will be stupefied as though put in a trance, which it will remain in for about ten minutes. Then lay it carefully in the long grass, get your dog and work him into the wind, towards where you know the bird to be. Try to time your dog's arrival at the bird to about ten minutes. The idea is that as the dog comes up to it, the bird, which has by now started to gain its equilibrium, jumps to its feet and flies away.

There is another method which I prefer, but which requires considerably more effort on your part, does not involve the dizzying of the bird and puts you in much greater control of the exact second the bird flushes. You are also in better control of flushing the bird, either yards in front of the dog, or quite literally right under its nose. The technique is referred to as the buried pigeon.

Spaniel winding pigeon.

Dig a small hole in the ground, which should be large enough to accommodate a pigeon with one wing fully opened, and should be deep enough so that the bird, when standing on the bottom of the hole, has his head about an inch below ground level. A piece of $\frac{1}{2}$-inch ply-wood, cut slightly larger than the hole, is slid over the top once the bird is in, with a long string (perhaps thirty yards) fastened through a hole you have drilled in the wood which is laid out downwind. The bird will remain there perfectly safely until you go and get your dog, and work him towards the hidden bird.

As he approaches where you know the bird to be secreted, pick up the string, and pull the lid away from the bird, which will immediately rocket skywards. As the bird flushes, blow your stop whistle. A little practice with this technique will quickly teach you how close to let your dog get to the bird before you flush it. You will also find that you can progressively flush the bird quite literally under the dog's nose. The bird of course flies back to its loft, completely unharmed, and can be used time after time.

Another obvious advantage of this technique is that since the bird is perfectly safely hidden and you do not have the limiting time factor of the dizzied pigeon, which will only remain dizzied for a short period of time, you can put out several birds on a circuit. In this way you can more closely simulate an actual day's shooting, flushing the birds at your leisure.

BRINGING IT ALL TOGETHER

As I have said in other chapters, you will have been building up your dog systematically over his whole training schedule, constantly going over everything that has been learnt to date as you add in each new aspect of his training. But now that your dog is dropping to flush and has reached this point in his train-ing, he is, to all intents and purposes, fully trained. His educa-tion is complete, but he is still not a gundog – that only comes with experience. You can liken your dog to a university grad-uate, or to an apprentice. Irrespective of how clever the indivi-dual is, regardless of how talented and adept at picking up education he is, it is the *experience* of working in the chosen profession that makes the student or apprentice complete.

In the case of your dog it is the real shooting field that will give him the experience that will develop him, over a couple of seasons, into the complete gundog that you can be proud of. But there is much that you can do to help your dog polish his training, to hone his reactions so that he is sharp, responsive and obedient.

The best way of going about the final training of your dog, when you can consolidate everything that you have taught him so far, is in a simulated shooting day. Leave your dog at home, or in the car, and set off with three live pigeons and half a dozen specimens of dead game in your bag – perhaps three rabbits and three pheasants, though in fact you can by now vary the game to anything that you have available. Lay out your set up, using as much imagination as you can, to give your dog as many different experiences as possible.

When you have secreted the retrieves and hidden the pigeons for flushing, return to your dog. To help you remember the exact location of the game it is a good idea to stick a small cane, sapling or twig near each hidden specimen, so that you have a guide to its location. There is nothing more annoying than discovering yourself unsure of exactly where you have left a hidden bird.

Shooting grouse from butt.

Dressed as though you were going for a day's shooting, carrying your gun, set off with your dog at heel. If he is a pointer or springer, you should be working him into the wind, in a nice tight and controlled pattern. Obviously any wild game that you flush is a bonus, and your dog should be 'bomb proof'. But the whole idea of using the game that you have hidden is that you can set your dog up whilst you are still in control, working the dog through his whole training regime of walking to heel, quartering, dropping when you stop, dropping to whistle, staying where he has dropped when you fire a shot, whilst you walk off and retrieve some imaginary piece of game. Return to him and either cast him out or walk him with you.

As you approach the first retrieve, try to slow down everything in your own mind, so that each aspect of the shot and retrieve is perfectly executed, with no sloppiness from either you or the dog. Fire a shot when the dog has his back to you and make sure he drops. Then after a short wait, work him out on to the retrieve. As he comes into the area where you know the game to be hidden, remember to give him that verbal aid when he is nearing the vicinity by calling 'steady'. Take the retrieve, which should be nicely presented, put it in your game bag, give him acknowledgement and work on. If you have alternated the retrieves and the flushes and if you have used your imagination on where you have hidden the dead game you should have a retrieve from cover, from across water, over a wall – in fact anywhere that your particular geography and imagination will allow. When you have completed the circuit, you have in fact gone through the whole of his training regime, and you will be able to see if there are any particular aspects of his training, any individual task, that needs greater emphasis. Then you can concentrate on improving and sharpening him up.

If, on the other hand, you feel completely satisfied with all aspects of his work, don't allow yourself to become complacent, but rather continue to polish his training on a regular basis up until the beginning of the shooting season, when wild game should supersede everything that has been organised and controlled so far. This type of training is based on the principle of an undisturbed and relatively painless progression from untrained puppyhood through to the working dog and if you keep to the schedule, by this time in his training, both you and the dog should thoroughly enjoy your trips outdoors working together.

8. GOING SHOOTING

Your dog's training schedule up until the day your first go shooting has been arranged in such a way that he has been systematically working towards the event in an increasingly more authentic pattern, so that he is well prepared for the day when you first take him shooting. In many ways you may almost have an anti-climax. If he has had thorough training he should take the first day's shooting in his stride, and any nerves will largely be your own.

However, there are several pitfalls in the shooting field that must be guarded against. No matter how well trained your dog is and no matter how good your control of him is, it is essential that you are aware of what to avoid. It would be most unwise ever to be tempted to take your young, inexperienced dog on a formal shoot, or on any shoot where several guns or dogs are likely to be, unless you do not have a gun and spend your time working the dog, giving it all your concentration, rather than trying to handle him whilst you shoot.

For his first day out it is a good idea to go with someone else, a friend who is a good shot. Leave your gun at home and have a day's rough shooting, when you concentrate on working your dog, while your friend shoots, since you must avoid runners. Obviously your dog is going to have to face the prospect of retrieving runners fairly soon, and there are a few simple but important guidelines to follow. Your dog must be made to drop to shot, and no matter how tempted you are, do not allow a young dog to chase a runner until it is well out of sight and preferably couched, before you set the dog after it. The dog, after all, does not know the difference between chasing a runner and chasing unshot game that runs away. Also, if the runner has run off and hidden, it gives your dog an ideal opportunity to practise his ability to take a line.

Wounded game that runs off and couches is more likely to

stiffen up as it bleeds internally, and is a great deal less likely to run off vigorously when the dog finally approaches. It is after all too much of a good thing to expect a young dog to know the difference between a fleeing animal which has been wounded, and a fleeing animal that it puts up as it works the ground. If you allow a young dog to pursue runners, then you are teaching the dog to chase and run in.

Equally serious runners to be avoided are pheasants. Anyone who has experienced pheasant shooting knows the surprising ability some pheasants have for running great distances before finally managing to hide. Therefore always try to stick to rabbits or game that is dead for your dog's first few shooting experiences.

The other very important reason why young dogs should not be allowed to go after runners is that up until now your dog has hopefully been encouraged to pick game gently – to be soft-mouthed. Then suddenly you send him out after a retrieve, and when he gets there he is faced with picking a struggling animal, and this can quickly result in the dog taking a firmer grip, squeezing the game and developing a hard mouth. Therefore, make it easy for the dog, and until he is experienced, try to restrict yourself to sending him on retrieves of dead game.

So tell your friend that if he is in any doubt that the quarry is dead, he should shoot it again, and for this reason it is advisable to stick to ground with a good rabbit population. A pheasant which comes down and is a runner is a great deal more difficult to shoot again – it's also a waste to have to put more lead into such a desirable bird for the table. Each time a rabbit is shot, make sure your dog has dropped, and leave him in a sitting position if the rabbit is visible and an easy retrieve, and pick the rabbit yourself. Try to make sure that all these early retrieves are from rabbits which the dog cannot see lying dead under its nose. It is much better to work him into a hidden rabbit and give both yourself and the dog plenty of time to work the ground.

Explain to your companion that since it is your dog's first day you intend to lay great emphasis on dog work and that you would appreciate his help and understanding. If your companion has a dog, unless it is impeccably trained, ask him if he would mind leaving it at home. It is most foolish to take a young dog into the field if there is the slightest chance of a badly trained dog running in, perhaps taking game from it, and generally competing with your dog.

You must of course accept that you will shoot in the company of another dog at some time, and the correct way to go about this is fairly simple. If you have a pointer or a spaniel, and the other fellow has a retriever, then allow your dog to work the ground, dropping to flush when game is shot. Now you are faced with a dilemma – which animal should be allowed to retrieve. The best course of action is to alternate the retrieve. Keep your dog sat, go up beside it so that you are standing fairly close and command it to sit, whilst the other dog is put on the retrieve, which it retrieves to its handler. Then continue on your way, working your dog. When the next piece of game is shot, both dogs should be commanded to sit, and then, standing well back from your companion and his dog, give your dog the command to retrieve. The reason you stand away from your companion and his dog is that some young dogs are reluctant to bring a retrieve too close to another dog, for fear that it will be taken away. So stand well to one side, take the retrieve, and by alternating in this fashion, you will prevent the dog getting the idea in his mind that every retrieve is automatically his property, as you enhance his good manners.

If you have a retriever and your companion has either a spaniel or a pointer, just reverse the procedure, keeping the dog working with you, under control, as he watches the other dog working, and alternate the retrieves. I must stress however, that if your companion has a dog which you are in any way doubtful about, you must be quite firm in your determination not to work your dog or expose it to the habits of the other dog. More good dogs are ruined by bad examples being set to them in the field than by probably any other single thing.

In an earlier chapter I drew the parallel between a young dog and any student getting its education, pointing out that experience is what makes a gundog, and you must remember that the experiences of the first season's work are largely what will govern your dog's attitude in the field in the years to come.

All experiences in the field during a dog's first season should be regarded as confidence and experience building. Commonsense must prevail, for after so much hard work you must observe caution if you are to prevent your dog becoming too fired up in the field, with the subsequent slackening of control and lack of sharpness in his reactions.

PICKING UP

Not for nothing do those who are particularly keen on dog work, and who compete in field trials, spend much time picking up, for I know of no better experience in the shooting field to tighten both you and your dog as a working team. It is picking up over a season which more than any other activity will teach you to read your dog's reactions, to fine tune your combined work together, and your control over the dog in a whole variety of difficult situations. Some people who are more used to shooting have a tendency to feel that picking up is a humble exercise, and this is very silly. Picking up is an integral part of the serious dog handler's year, and opportunities should be sought out and capitalised on.

Approach the head keeper, or shoot captain of your nearest large shoot, and honestly explain to him that you have a young dog you would like to give the opportunity of picking game. Whilst most shooters are usually only too delighted to have someone with a good dog, make it clear that it is picking up you want to do, and not beating, since while picking up is an excellent aid to your training, beating can have distinctly the opposite effect. The spaniel which has never experienced the exhilaration of other dogs, abundant game, and the general commotion of beaters and guns is almost guaranteed to become over-heated and as soon as you enter the covet and he is cast he is highly likely to be tempted to draw you that bit further. Aided by the general excitement from the other dogs the dog can, to the owner's dismay, appear to have completely forgotten all his training as he charges about out of control. So if beating is all that is offered to you, do not be tempted to use a young and inexperienced dog, unless it is kept on the lead, and is taken along purely as a spectator, not a participant.

When you arrive on the day to pick up, it is well to go through the following few formalities which will not only single you out as being entirely serious about your dog work, but will also give you infinitely superior results with your dog.

When you first arrive at the meeting place where the shoot is gathering, if you have an estate car, open the back of the car, and command the dog to sit. Leaving the back of the car open, with the dog remaining where it is, join the other beaters and pickers up for the day. Introduce yourself to the head keeper, and let him know of your arrival. Keep an eye on your dog, who should remain sitting in the back of the car.

A typical scene on such occasions is one of relative confusion, as the guests, beaters, and pickers up arrive. There is the inevitable jumble of dogs charging this way and that, sniffing each other, lifting their legs against every car wheel and fence post, and generally enjoying a form of canine communal fun. It must be remembered however, that these dogs are at this time out of the control of their owners, and this is when the general excitement of the day starts to build within the dog. Much better to keep your dog sitting quietly in the back of the car, until the shoot is ready to move off, when you get the dog, and, keeping it at heel and under control, go to your allotted peg.

Empty gun through fence with black labrador.

If you have arrived at a shoot and you do not have a car which facilitates leaving the dog sitting in the back as a spectator, or if your dog is an excitable type of animal, then as an alternative, keep it on the lead as you introduce yourself to the other pickers up. What you are trying to avoid is letting your dog, even for the shortest time, be out of your control.

A perfect example of this is illustrated by a gentleman who bought a dog from me. This particular dog was exceptionally well trained and 100% reliable in every aspect of his training. As a personality he was calm and quiet with a complete absence of any nonsense, drawing all his pleasure from working well. He had experienced two seasons working as my own dog, and it could be fairly claimed that he was exceptional in every way.

His new owner telephoned me two or three times in the months after he had taken over the dog, to tell me how pleased he was with the dog. He was a shoot captain of a large and exclusive pheasant syndicate, and had to have quite simply the best dog, free of all vices, and beyond any form of criticism, since it fell to him to have to order the other guns if they did not have excellent dogs, to leave them behind.

He telephoned me after he had had his dog some three months into the shooting season to tell me of a minor problem that was developing, and ask my advice. Apparently when sent on a retrieve the dog had, on one or two occasions, deviated and run some fifteen or twenty yards to the next dog working on a parallel retrieve and had a quick sniff, before resuming his work on a command from his owner. I found this behaviour puzzling as I knew that this dog had never before been tempted to commit even this seemingly small and unimportant misdemeanour.

After questioning the gentleman about his routine from leaving the house, I recognised the danger area. Although the owner's home was less than an hour's drive from the shoot, when he arrived, he thought it only fair that the dog should be let out of the car to relieve himself. So for that short period of perhaps only ten minutes or so I discovered that whilst the owner was engaged in conversation with the other guns, he was allowing the dog to move freely amongst the other dogs, to join the general mêlée and indulge himself in the delights of a communal sniff. Unwittingly, the new owner, having allowed his dog to enjoy this small freedom, had taught him to pay attention to other dogs that came into his immediate proximity. I suggested that he stop allowing the dog to intermingle in this fashion, and the problem quickly stopped.

Walk with your dog to the peg or area where you have been told to position yourself. If the gun has a dog, ask him if he intends using it, although this would be unlikely. Place yourself well behind the gun. If you are on a grouse moor, sixty yards is all that should be necessary, whereas with high driven pheasants, particularly if the shoot is on hilly countryside, it may be necessary for you to stand 100 yards behind the gun. Make sure he knows where you are. The actual distance you stand will be dictated by the type of shooting and configuration of the ground.

Some people prefer to let all the birds fall and the drive be over before they start picking game. Personally I prefer to work the dog on each bird as it falls. You quickly get into the habit of working your dog on a retrieve while you count the birds that fall behind the gun. Pay particular attention to strong runners, birds that may be shot possibly in one wing and obviously are far from dead, and take note in which direction they have gone. Then as soon as the drive is over, pick these birds first. It is because of the possibility of strong runners that it is best not to take a young dog picking up too early in its shooting career. It may even be necessary, in the case of some runners, to get your dog away to it immediately, although this should only be done with an experienced dog.

If you are fortunate enough to be picking up on a shoot where a lot of birds are expected to be shot, it is no bad thing to take with you a sheet of paper and a pencil. Mark the top of the page with a circle indicating your gun, and further down the page, another circle, indicating yourself. Then, as each bird falls, indicate the location with a small ×. This avoids confusion, and means that you have a greater chance of picking every bird. If however, when you are picking up, you notice another dog is obviously on the same retrieve as your dog, stop your dog immediately and call it in. Otherwise you risk a tug of war.

At the end of the day, remember to thank the keeper. He has after all done you a favour, and if you have played your part in the day's proceedings and your dog has behaved, then both of you are assured of being invited to subsequent shoots.

WILDFOWLING

The one area of retrieving where it may occasionally be necessary for you to get your dog away speedily on a retrieve, rather than keep him sitting for a short spell before being sent out, is that of wildfowling. Water birds which are wounded have an alarming ability of being able to dive right in front of a dog, to reappear some twenty yards further on, and can cause a young dog to swim around and around in cold water on a futile pursuit of a bird which he has little chance of retrieving, while at the same time burning up much-needed energy. So if you are shooting geese or duck, and a bird comes down that you think is not dead, it is advisable to get the dog away quickly, since in most cases a wounded bird, a goose for example, will often appear stunned for a few seconds after it has hit the water before it gains its equilibrium and, on seeing the dog's approach,

Shooting geese from hide, accompanied by retriever.

starts to dive. So get your dog away immediately so that with luck he will be on to the bird before it starts to dive.

If you send a dog on a retrieve on a bird which starts to dive, and your dog starts to swim after it, then you will see the benefit of having spent so much time doing his advanced water work with dummies. In every shooting man's career, there comes a time when he must decide whether it is best to lose a bird, and allow it to get away wounded, than to risk his dog swimming endlessly back and forwards in freezing water until it becomes exhausted, and is likely to drown. It is for that very reason that you must have been particularly diligent in the control of your dog and calling it off a retrieve. If, however, you are ever faced with the prospect of putting your dog on a retrieve quickly, sometimes even before the bird has hit the water, as may be the case if you have seen a goose coming down with one broken wing, then remember that the next two or three retrieves must be well controlled. Keep the dog in a sitting position for several minutes before you send it on a retrieve so that you enforce control.

If you are ever faced with a situation where you must call your dog off a retrieve and leave a wounded bird, then you owe it not only to the bird, but to the good name of field sportsmen, to return the next morning and search for the bird. It will often be found dead, or at least a lot less active than in the previous evening's flight.

When shooting at any flood water, always remember to check for the presence of submerged fences, which can be seen as the line of the fence comes out of the water, and either work your dog from an area where he is not going to encounter a submerged fence or if necessary, don't shoot, since a dog, no matter how experienced, when swimming in water (particularly if it is dark), has no way of knowing how to negotiate a fence which he comes against.

It makes good sense that you always pay attention to your dog's physical condition, and the little extra effort it requires to towel him dry at the end of the day will bring its own rewards. Do not ever expect a dog, irrespective of how tough and hardy you think he is, to have worked hard on a cold rainy day and then to have endured either a wet journey home or being put into a kennel, wet and cold, without running the serious risk of all the maladies that can be brought on in later years with such a lack of consideration.

Always dry your dog before putting him away for the night. If you have travelled by car to a shoot, dry him before you put him in the car. If it is cold weather, or you expect him to be wet and cold, the sensible, caring dog owner will take with him a small nourishing snack, which he can feed the dog from the back of the car.

Black labrador retrieving mallard duck through decoys.

A technique which I have used for many years, and I think has much to commend it, is having a large bag which I have sewn up with a drawstring around the top. The bag is sufficiently large to put the whole dog inside and drawstring it loosely around his neck. In this fashion the dog remains warm, as the excess moisture comes out of his skin and is absorbed by the bag during the journey home. This indulgence is entirely for the dog's benefit. It is a small bonus that it also keeps the car clean.

SCENTS

Since men began working with dogs, it has been taken for granted that their more developed scenting powers allow them to follow invisible scent lines, which are beyond our abilities to detect. But an understanding of what scent really is will help the gundog trainer to understand the many and varied problems which your dog may have to face on any particular shooting day.

Dogs fall into two different categories: ground scenters and air scenters. The air scenting dog, such as the GSP, will primarily follow scents which are above the ground, and this can be seen by the dog running with his head up. Ground scenters predominantly find their scents on the ground, and this can be seen by a labrador following a line, his nose skimming and searching close to the soil. But ground or air scenters are only better in one aspect of scenting – an air scenter can follow a ground scent and vice versa.

CONDITIONS

Weather conditions play an important part in whether a scent is strong or weak. You will often hear, whenever there is talk of gundogs and dog work, the comment that it was a bad scenting day. This is not an excuse. There are days when scenting conditions appear to be ideal, the scent remaining for a considerable time after the passage of an animal or bird. On a windy day any air scent will dissipate quickly. On a very hot day, the scent will tend to rise and disperse in air currents. Obviously in heavy rain a scent will be suppressed and quickly dilute. The best scenting conditions are crisp, warm days, with a light breeze, to give the dog direction.

WHAT IS SCENT?

Scent is made up of a variety of different constituents. As your dog's nose becomes educated to discern and filter the different smells, he learns how to discard the unimportant and unwanted smells and concentrate on the different odours that guide him to the line taken. A bird or animal whether it is a cock pheasant or a rabbit, has a distinctive odour, and as it passes across or through vegetation it will leave small scent molecules in the air. It will add to the channel of smells, disturbed leaves, broken grasses, small seemingly unimportant smells which all unite into a distinctive trail.

Most of us only ever come across the question of scent when our gundog is sent after a runner, and this is where the scent is likely to be much stronger. How, for instance, does a dog know how to follow a line of one particular wounded pheasant that may have run through cover which contains several other birds? It is because of the chemical group known as feremones. We have all heard the old wives' tale that a dog knows if you are afraid of it. This is quite true. The dog also knows if you are not afraid of it. It is given this information by the scent given off by your skin glands, over which you have no control. They register your mood, and the dog, with his highly attuned scenting capabilities, instinctively knows whether the scent means fear, aggression, confidence or whatever.

So the pheasant which has been pricked, which comes to earth with a bump, is giving off a distinctive odour of alarm, or fear and it is wrong to suggest that it is either the smell of the shot having struck the bird, or the smell of blood. I have heard both of these suggestions put forward, and both have no scientific basis. A pricked bird seldom bleeds, at least for some considerable distance, but it does know that something is wrong and as it runs off to hide it obviously has some degree of anxiety, and this trail is easily followed by the experienced nose of a gundog.

A good way of seeing how obvious a smell channel is can often be witnessed as your dog becomes more experienced in his training. Watch him as he nears the area where you have hidden a dummy. He will cast backwards and forwards into the wind. Sometimes, if the wind is swirling, he will show the distinct sign that he has smelt something, and start to run towards the hidden dummy. Then he may stop – he has lost the smell – and cast backwards and forwards before he re-locates it, and runs along the invisible track to the hidden retrieve.

9. TRIALS AND TRIALING

Field trials and working tests are a very important aspect of the gundog scene, and it is through the ever-changing world of trialing dogs that we keep the high standard of work and abilities in the best of our dogs. Gundog owners fall into two categories, the shooting man who has a working dog as a necessary extension to his sport; and the dog man who shoots – the individual who is prepared to put much more work into his gundog and who gets a great deal of reward from training and working him. It is the man more orientated to dog work who is likely to enjoy trialing, which can be a very rewarding experience. However, most gundogs never see a trial, their owners being content to have the dog purely for their own interest and sport, being disinterested in any form of competition. This is unfortunate, since a healthy competitive spirit can only improve the gundog trainer's appreciation of his dog, and has the distinct advantage of encouraging the trainer to continue to strive for higher standards.

If you want to try competing, then it is as well to prepare yourself and your dog. You must remember that the field trialing world, like any other community, has its personalities, its likes and dislikes, and it is a fact of life that your face must fit. Therefore you should always approach any group of trialing enthusiasts as very much the new boy, and whatever you do, don't for a moment assume that either of you are going to set the heather alight, or win straightway, irrespective of how good you think your dog is. However, most experienced trialing men and women are only to pleased to see new faces, and are always willing to give help and advice, if asked.

This chapter is intended to give you a general guide as to what to expect at field trials, but no book can substitute for the experience of going to several trials as a spectator and fully experiencing the day. Don't be afraid to ask what the form is,

Hen grouse with chicks.

nor that matter to take notes, and you will find that after a few enjoyable days as a spectator you will be better prepared to take both your dog and yourself into the arena. It is far better to do this than stay away and try to do all your preparations from books.

If you think that you will have any intention of trialing you should approach the field trial society relevant to your dog's breed as soon as possible. You must also have registered your dog with the Kennel Club, which you should do anyway, if you want to do anything with the dog whether it be breeding or trialing. Start going to trials before your dog is old enough to enter, and you will see the sort of standard that your dog will have to achieve if it is going to have a reasonable chance of success.

The work required of dogs in trials is really only a refined and highly polished and compacted version of what is expected of a dog in the shooting field, so don't be put off or intimidated and think you may not be good enough. Just prepare your dog and work on his training using as experience everything you have observed at the different events you have visited. If you have joined the relevant society, visited trials and let it be known that you intend to enter your dog, you will have a greater chance of having your dog accepted for a place. Often, more dogs are entered than can possibly be accommodated in the time allotted and so, as a general rule, new members have to wait until the more established members of the society are drawn.

PREPARING THE DOG

You will be expected to work with your dog, giving a minimum of commands and assistance so it is better if you spend considerable time sharpening up your dog and his communication with you. Treat him like an athlete. It is virtually impossible to keep any animal at peak condition all the time, and therefore in the weeks prior to any event, put greater emphasis on his physical fitness as well as his work. If you are starting to give your dog additional exercise by working him hard, then it is necessary to step up his protein intake so that you achieve peak condition, both mentally and physically, in time for the event.

Nothing tires a dog more than a long car journey prior to being taken out and expected to perform. So you must make a decision. If the event you are entering is far enough away to justify an overnight stay then this is a wise decision. Then, on the morning of the event both you and the dog will be bright-eyed and bushy-tailed and that much more prepared for the day's activity. In many ways it is a case of psyching yourself up. If you decide to drive, on the same day, then it is always wise to leave early in the morning so that you get there in plenty of time which will give you time to relax.

On the morning of the trial, give your dog a light, high-protein breakfast, and a restricted exercise period of not more than fifteen to twenty minutes. It is too late to start adding any last minute lessons. You have committed yourself and it is preferable you do no work at this stage with your dog, but rather concentrate on both of you relaxing. Certainly try to avoid taking the whole business too seriously. Luck has as much to do with winning as in any other competitive activity. Most important, at all costs try to avoid tension or nerves. Your dog will quickly pick up your attitude and neither of you will give of your best.

When you arrive at the trial location, keep your dog on the lead, irrespective of whether it is the best and most obedient animal that was ever born. You should be seen to be doing the right thing. Find the secretary or organiser of the day, introduce yourself and inform him of the number you have been allotted. Unless you are one of the first few dogs to run, retire and join the other competitors amongst the watching audience, and enjoy the event.

FIELD TESTS

An excellent guide to the sort of competition, control and experience of the whole test and trial business is for you to enter your dog in several field tests before you ever consider higher things. A field test is very simple, and is purely a test of the basic requirements of any working dog, where you will be expected to do no more than you would do in any training exercise. Dogs are given a series of simple retrieves, always on dummies, and with no unmarked retrieves. The other advantage of field tests is that the dog is expected to perform on its own, without the additional distraction of another working with him. There are many field tests run throughout the country and they do not involve nearly as much officialdom as trials. You do not, for instance, have to be a member of the society, since most field tests are run by gun clubs and local field sports organisations.

Redleg partridge.

The natural progression from field test is the novice trial, and whilst you will be expected to work with live game, novice trials are not susceptible to anything like the pressure, tensions and feelings of high competition in an open trial. During a novice trial there is a general, more relaxed atmosphere, and the judges have as their criteria the standard one would expect from a young and less experienced dog, and are therefore much less demanding and more forgiving. It is through the natural progression of tests and novice trials that both you and your dog are eventually refined, tuned and prepared for the much more demanding work of the trial.

SPANIEL TRIALS

In spaniel trials there are two judges who judge one dog apiece – therefore two spaniels work simultaneously. As your turn in the trial approaches, the steward will indicate to you that you should come to the front. Whatever you do, do not leap forward, pre-guessing the judge's requirements. Remain behind him until he asks you to take your place in the line. At that time you should take the lead from your dog, take your place, and the trial begins.

The dogs will be required to hunt vigorously for the two guns who walk on either side of you. Be diligent in making sure that your dog works his ground efficiently, that he goes right to the outside edges of his allotted avenue or area. Watch carefully. The instant the dog flushes, peep the stop whistle. If the game is shot, wait until the judge indicates whether he would prefer your dog to retrieve the game or not. Do not assume that he will expect a retrieve. Wait until he asks you.

While your dog is working, if you hear a shot being fired from the other end of the line, over the other dog, drop your dog immediately, using your whistle. Here a slightly difficult question may arise. The other judge may decide he does not want his dog to retrieve this particular piece of game, and if you have not yet had an opportunity to have a retrieve your judge may well ask you if you would like to take it. Whilst it is not obligatory that you take a retrieve shot down the line, it is good manners to do so. However, do not send your dog out before you have ascertained exactly where the retrieve lies. The sense of this is quite obvious. There is little point in trying to work your dog on a blind retrieve when you have only a faint indication of its location.

Do not permit yourself any show of frustration or anger. Never resort to shouting, and try at all times when you are in the field to act the very model of the perfect dog handler, whether your dog is misbehaving or not.

Eventually the judge will feel that he has assessed your dog, and indicate to you that for the moment at least he is finished with you. Put your dog on the lead and drop back amongst the followers. Irrespective of whether your dog has behaved brilliantly or done everything wrong, stay calm.

Springer spaniel with cock pheasant.

Eventually you will be called forward again, this time to work for the second judge. The time between your first and second run can vary. If there have been a number of eliminations, you may well be called on pretty soon, so don't vanish off back to the car for a reviving cup of coffee. Stay on hand, show interest in the proceedings, and be there so that when you are called you can step forward immediately. The run you will be expected to work with your dog under the second judge should be similar to the first.

If you discover that luck has not been with you that day and that you have been eliminated, accept the judges' decision, and whatever you do, do not be tempted to enter into discussion or argument. Equally, if you find that you are amongst the winners, accept the situation gracefully. In your next trial you may well discover you fail miserably.

Remember that under the excitement of the day things may well go wrong, and no matter how frustrating it is when your dog commits some misdemeanor that you know is certainly not typical, it is the actions on that particular day that the judges are looking for. They are not only looking for style, general work and response to handling, but also the dog's abilities to generally carry out the work expected of the breed. You will be disqualified if the dog chases game, fails on a retrieve, damages game, barks, whines or generally gives tongue, runs over ground missing game, lifts and retrieves unshot game, and does not give up the retrieve on command. You will also be disqualified if the dog runs in, either to the fall of game or shot.

When all the dogs have run and the trial has finished the judges, who will have been taking notes on the performances, will confer. If they are not in agreement as to the winning dogs, then it is normal for them to ask for a run-off. This would involve three or four dogs, who would all be expected to run at the same time, giving the judges a better opportunity to watch all the dogs working at the same time. From this run-off the judges would make a decision. Finally, certificates are presented and general congratulations handed out. Whether you are amongst the winners or not, both you and your dog will have learned much from the experience, so that when you return to your next trial you will both be better prepared for whatever you are asked to do.

RETRIEVER TRIALS

The type of work and performances required at retriever trials differs in many ways from the expected tasks of a spaniel trial. The main difference is of course, that a retriever is not expected to hunt game. It is because he is a specialist retriever that particular emphasis will be put on all aspects of his retrieving, and the judges will be expecting, and should get, a very high standard of control in this aspect of dog work.

Your retriever will be expected, when not called on to work, to stay happily and confidently at heel, and act like a gentleman. The work required of a retriever in a trial is slightly different from what is expected and wanted of their dogs by the majority of retriever owners, and in this slight difference the two types of dog are worlds apart.

The average rough shooting retriever owner prefers his dog to hunt in front of him. Certainly he will not do it as effectively as a spaniel or an HPR dog, but unless your shooting is exclusively driven, when you stand at a peg, almost all retriever owners will have encouraged their dogs to hunt and flush, and drop to flush, albeit at fairly close range.

Conversely, trialing dogs are not expected to hunt in any way, but to be able to carry out long, difficult retrieves, where there is great emphasis placed on the handler's ability to work the dog out on these distant retrieves, to the exclusion of all other distractions, either furred or feathered, that might be in the dog's path. If a retriever's natural instinct to hunt has been developed and refined, if he has been trained to work that bit closer to the handler, then he will be less prepared to work on very long, blind retrieves.

Therefore the preparation of a retriever for a trial will involve greater emphasis on your hand signals, and you would do well to dwell diligently on the chapter in this book which describes the use of walls and fences to give your dog experience on long, straight runs on command, whether it be left, right, or straight back. Once a retriever has experienced the idea that if you continually wave him in a particular direction, albeit for several hundred yards, he will be rewarded by finding a retrieve, then he will have greater confidence in following your signal. It is after all only a distance barrier that you have to break and once the dog has got it into his head that when you line him up, set him on a course and send him away, that the peep of your whistle and the command of steady results in him making a find, then the distance work should present little problems.

Similar to all other forms of trial, retriever trials are in front of an audience, with other dogs working there. It is therefore imperative that you pay attention to your dog being confident when others are about and make sure he learns to ignore other dogs. To teach him this take your dog to the local clay pigeon club, keep him on the lead and stand well back when you first introduce him to this new experience of people, noise and shouting. Progressively move closer, until you are standing behind one of the busiest stands, with the dog sitting at your heel watching the proceedings. Discourage anyone from making a fuss of your dog in this situation by simply telling them that you are there to give your dog experience of ignoring others.

There is one other little technique you can employ if you want to seriously go into trials. You will notice that the majority of participants and the audience are dressed in variations of Barbour coats, caps and green wellies. From a distance such a panoply tends to take on a general uniformity to the dog's eye, in shades of monochrome. So give your dog a little help. When he has run out on a long retrieve, when he looks back at you for direction, or when he has picked the retrieve and turns on the return, it makes it that little bit easier for him if you wear something distinctive, whether it be a lighter-coloured coat, a yellow waistcoat, or some equally noticeable garment. Of course, you would have to wear this whenever you were training the dog. One eminent gundog trainer I know wears a garish tartan cap when he trials. It may be a small help, but it certainly is worth considering.

There is another training exercise that you should pay attention to with a dog which you intend to trial. Get a friend to remain in cover, about 200 yards away. You stand quietly with your dog sitting at heel. On your pre-arranged signal your companion fires a shot to draw the dog's attention, whilst simultaneously throwing a dummy high in the air to catch the dog's eye. Wait a short time, then squat beside your dog, line him up and send him out. In this way you will teach your dog to watch for and mark distant retrieves which would not be typical of normal shooting. After he has perfected this form of retrieving then you would naturally move on to having your friend hide a second dummy to either left or right of the thrown dummy (in the initial stages not more than thirty yards) and when your dog nears the first marked retrieve, stop him on the whistle and hand direct him to the hidden retrieve.

The judges will of course be assessing the dog's style, marking capabilities, ability to take directions and retrieve beautifully to hand – and all this to be carried out with a minimum of noise. They will also be looking for speed, style, and the general set of the dog, his carriage and flair. He will be eliminated if he barks or gives tongue, if he damages game, is hard mouthed, if he runs in, refuses to enter or cross water, or goes out of control. He will also be eliminated if he changes birds. Whilst it is not allowed for a dog to drop a bird during a retrieve, it is entirely permissible and acceptable if, after his initial collection, he lays the bird down to get a better grip and balance of the retrieve.

One thing you never do in any trial is try to hoodwink the judge. If, for instance, your dog brings you a bird which you think may be damaged, do not try turning your back on the judge as you take the retrieve and quickly try to smooth down the feathers. Most judges have seen just about every trick in the book and are fully aware that birds can be damaged during the fall, particularly if it has hit either stony or frozen ground. If you know your dog is not hard mouthed, yet it brought back a torn bird, it is far wiser to point out to the judge that the bird is damaged and that you think it unlikely that it was caused by your dog. Certainly the judge will be scrupulous in his attention on your next retrieve, but that is only fair.

A retriever trial would normally involve three or four judges walking in line. In the case of three judges, each one has the responsibility to judge two dogs working in front of him, making it six dogs running in the trial at any one time. In the case of four judges, they would normally work in pairs and only four dogs would be put forward together.

Once you have been called into the line, take your place, and as the line moves forward, game will be put up and shot. The judges will indicate which dog they wish to take the retrieve. Do not assume anything. Do only as the judges request you to do. It doesn't matter if the bird is nearest to you and perfect for your dog, which has marked it beautifully. The judges have the overall picture to consider, and may well decide that retrieves should be taken by dogs further up or down the line. Throughout the whole procedure your dog should be sitting quietly at your side, giving no signs of anxiety. He shouldn't fidget or make a sound but happily watch the other dogs working in front of him. If you are asked to take an unmarked retrieve from further down the line, it is imperative that you pay attention to the wind direction before you send your dog out, and direct him downwind of where you know the game to be before working him on to the retrieve. When the judge is satisfied that he has seen sufficient from your dog he will tell you, and you may rejoin the audience. During your second run, although you will be under a different judge, the procedure will usually be exactly the same.

If you are at a trial which involves a drive, your dog will be expected to behave as he would or should during any formal day's shooting. He must sit patiently and quietly, observing the shooting going on around him, and must not be tempted to move as the birds fall around him. Even if a runner passes within a few feet of him he must make no attempt to move after it.

HPR TRIALS

As the various different breeds of HPR dogs have become more popular so too have the trials and tests and it is becoming an increasingly competitive field. Also, as the competition is increasing so is the quality of the work seen at these events.

An HPR trial is really little different from what would be expected of the dog on a normal well-run shooting day. The dogs are run singly under two judges, and the dog is expected to work in front of normally two or even three guns walking in line.

When you are called forward to take your place, go forward to the judge, take the lead off the dog and cast it forward. The HPR is expected to quarter the line diligently so make sure he goes right to the far edges of the space allotted. As he turns and quarters the ground, he should do so with flair and confidence, coming on a point rock steady, and holding it until the gun has put himself in a position where he is ready to shoot. The dog should then flush on command, and remain exactly where he is until told to retrieve. If, after the game has been flushed, it flies off unscathed, the dog must immediately resume his quartering on command.

Because of the diverse abilities of the HPR dogs, they can be generally much more interesting to watch since the trial will

German shorthaired pointer gives perfect sitting retrieve of greylag goose.

involve different types of terrain which test the dogs as fully as possible in each type of environment. The dog would be expected to work through light woodland and either over open arable land or moorland and obviously would be expected to do at least one water retrieve.

As I have said, luck plays an enormous part in trailing. But it is a highly interesting and exciting extension of your dog work, and perseverance and hard work with your dog will normally bring results.

10. BITCHES AND BREEDING

Everyone who owns a bitch has to face the question of whether to breed from her, and many taproom experts are only too prepared to give opinions as to the relative value of having a litter of puppies and make all sorts of claims about the various benefits such an exercise would give. These claims, however, are normally fanciful and not based on any true scientific knowledge. So, is it beneficial for a bitch to have puppies? The answer is simple, the benefits of having them can be outweighed by the problems that may be caused by having them. In other words, the one cancels out the other.

It certainly appears that a bitch which has had a litter is less likely to have trouble with her uterus in later years, but there can also be adverse effects caused by having a litter. However, it must be accepted that bitches come into season, normally twice a year, and it is just bad luck if she manages to time this in the middle of the shooting season. Some bitches can be worked for the first week of their season, so long as they are working on their own, or in the company of other bitches. But if there is a dog about, the whole exercise becomes rather silly, since even the best trained dogs hastily forget their training once they get wind of the compelling scent of a bitch in season. So if you have a bitch that has come into heat during the shooting season, leave her at home.

There are of course several tablets and sprays available from both the chemist and your vet. However, they are not the cure-all, acting more as a disuader to dogs hanging around your door, and would certainly not provide protection that you could rely on during a day's shooting. Also, some bitches when they come into season, seem to lose all semblance of sense, appearing to want to do nothing more than remain by their owner's side, or worse, particularly after a bitch has been served before. In that instance there is a greater compunction for her to follow her natural instincts. One GSP bitch I trained was throughout the year absolutely superb and in every way 100% reliable as a good, solid, working dog. Yet when she came into season she appeared to lose all control of her senses. She was not only unwilling to work but appeared unhappy if she got any further than a few yards from my side. This particular bitch was not even prepared to sit in a car if I left her for a short time, but would make every effort to get out of the vehicle in her desire to stay with me.

SEASONS

Normally you will get plenty of warning that your bitch is coming into season. Her vulva will swell quite noticeably and small drops of blood and fluid will start to appear. Some bitches are quite vigorous in their efforts to keep themselves clean, continually licking and washing themselves, whilst others seem less interested, allowing themselves to become quite soiled. A season lasts, on average, for twenty-one days, and if you were intending to have puppies then you must watch the bitch carefully.

About ten days after the beginning of her season the fluid discharge will change colour and become clearer. If you intend to have the bitch served, it is between the tenth and thirteenth day, that conception is most likely to take place. The fluid will continue to seep until the end of her season. If, during your bitch's season, there is the slightest possibility that she may have been caught by a dog, and you want to avoid the chance of an unwanted pregnancy, take her immediately to the vet who will give her the appropriate injection.

TO MATE OR NOT TO MATE

Irrespective of whether you have what you think is a good bitch or not, everyone who has a gundog has a responsibility to behave correctly and to try at all times to maintain a high standard of dog stock. You must be honest with yourself and not fall into the temptation of having a litter for either financial or emotional reasons. If your dog is a poor specimen, if it suffers from any hereditary defect such as being under or over-shot, you have a duty not to have puppies from it, otherwise you are perpetuating the very problem that so many people interested in gundogs work hard to eradicate. However, if you are absolutely determined to have a puppy from your bitch, and it is not of good breeding stock nor an excellent specimen, then the least you can do is not to issue a pedigree with the puppies, making it absolutely clear to any potential buyer, as well as to the owner of the stud dog, that this is your intention.

FALSE PREGNANCY

If you are not familiar with the condition of false pregnancy, it can be quite alarming, and an understanding of what is happening to your bitch will help you to know how to react. False pregnancy is not an uncommon occurrence, and can take the form of a simple swelling of the abdomen, usually six to nine weeks after she has been in season. This swelling may last a few days and then recede but in other dogs it may continue to grow, almost as though the dog was genuinely pregnant, until eventually the animal becomes quite broody and may even start to prepare a nest, as though a litter of pups was imminent. A bitch in this condition will often take possession of some piece of familiar household equipment – it can be a child's doll, or even an old slipper, and she will direct all her maternal instincts towards it and appear to treat it exactly as she would a puppy, carrying it about and being highly possessive.

If your bitch starts to develop a false pregnancy condition, it is the wisest course to take her straight to the vet who will prescribe a course of tablets. Whatever you do, don't be tempted just to let the condition take its course. You can cause the bitch considerable suffering, confusion, and mental upset. You can greatly help a bitch that comes into this condition if you make sure that she has plenty of exercise, is not allowed unlimited liquid and is kept away from heat.

SPAYING

Spaying is another subject that suffers a great deal from a lack of public knowledge, and although it may be unnecessary to even include it in a book on gundogs, since it is unlikely that anyone who has gone to the expense and effort to get a bitch would want her reproductive system rendered useless, I feel it is relevant to discuss the subject, to avoid misunderstandings. Though the operation is a relatively simple exercise for any vet, and has the advantages that the bitch will no longer come into season or be susceptible to uterine problems in years to come, it is not, in my personal opinion, a course of action that should be advised. If you choose a bitch you should accept the responsibility of the animal and its gender, rather than try to avoid the minor inconveniences by resorting to surgery.

Some people claim that they prefer the more mellow temperament that can be induced by spaying, but to me this is an excuse, purely reflecting the owner's inability to cope with the dog. It is a widely held belief that after spaying bitches become fat and lethargic. This is certainly not true. A spayed bitch has in general a more mellow temperament, and consequently requires less food. Just like humans, the only way a dog will become fat and lethargic is by eating more food than the exercise it takes justifies.

CASTRATION

There is no reason that can possibly justify ever considering having a dog castrated, other than severe aggressiveness or if your dog habitually runs away, straying in search of pastures new. Although in some cases castration might cure these problems it should rarely be considered. Rather than resorting to surgery to try and improve an undesirable dog, it is infinitely preferable to start again with a better and more desirable puppy.

MATING

At its simplest, breeding of dogs can be left to a bitch in season and the nearest dog. They will get on with it, without any assistance, and in due course pups will probably appear. However, anyone who is seriously interested in gundogs and is considering either allowing their dog to be used to serve a bitch or having puppies from their bitch, has several considerations they must take into account. If you possess a dog, and someone asks you to oblige them with a service, you must ask yourself if your dog is an excellent specimen, or does he possess any faults which are undesirable. Having satisfied yourself that your dog is suitable then you must apraise the bitch and ask the same questions about her, for there is little point in perpetuating undesirable physical or character faults. It is too easy to be greedy, and everyone who is interested in gundogs has a responsibility to make every effort to do their part to keep dogs as near to the standard of the breed as possible.

Once you have satisfied yourself that both dogs are suitable, then you must examine their pedigrees and make sure that they do not have too many common recent ancestors. If you are in doubt as to the pedigrees' suitability, then any competent dog breeder or vet could easily advise you.

If you have a good quality bitch, then rather than just using any handy dog of the same breed, it is preferable to book a service with a top quality field trials champion. In this way you take a great deal of the guesswork out of the union, and of course have a much greater chance of getting a better price for the puppies and passing on a much better canine product.

The use of a dog from a professional kennel has many things to recommend it. First of all, if you are inexperienced in the actual mating process, it doesn't matter, since the dog's owner will handle the whole affair, being more used to it. Book your service well in advance, since the owner of the stud dog will certainly have to satisfy himself that your bitch is suitable and also slot her into the calendar so that he doesn't have too many bitches arriving at the same time.

The standard practice with professionals is to charge a flat fee. Again this is preferable than the sort of arrangement that often takes place between two friends who are going to use their own dogs. In this case the standard arrangement is that the owner of the dog will take the pick of the litter. However, I advise against this practice. It works well only if your bitch has several puppies. However, I have known of cases where a bitch has had one or two pups. The owner of the dog has taken his as arranged, leaving the owner of the bitch in the unenviable position of having had all the work and ending up with only one, or even no pups. So it is preferable that you agree a fee with the owner of the dog and make sure that whatever arrangements you come to, everything is agreed before the service takes place.

It is ill-advised to consider taking a litter of puppies from your bitch before she is adult and her training complete, and certainly not before her second birthday. Try to time the mating so that the puppies will be born during the spring or summer months. This makes everything so much easier. The temperature is warmer and it gives the pups a better start than having to cope with the cold and wet, as they would if they were born later in the year.

Watch your bitch coming into season. From the first signs that her season has started, you have ten to twelve days to wait before she will reach the stage where conception is most likely. Watch the colour of the fluid discharge from her vulva, and when it starts to change colour, this is the best time to introduce her to the dog. Depending on the bitch, the best time for conception is between the tenth and thirteenth day. You should give the dog owner advance warning of the season's start so he will know to within a day when you are best to introduce the two dogs.

When you do this they may immediately get down to the business, or the bitch may skip about for a little while before standing for the dog, with her tail to one side. If she is not prepared to stand, then you may be a day too early, although in the case of some bitches who have not previously been served if you are absolutely certain of your dates it may be necessary to hold her firmly to allow the dog to mount. This course of action however is not to be recommended, since very often your presence will disturb the bitch and she will be more concerned with keeping her attention on you than on the business in hand.

The best course of action, unless both dogs immediately show signs of enthusiasm for each other, is to put them in a quiet run where they will not be disturbed, and retire out of sight, where you can keep your eye on them discreetly. After the dog has mounted the bitch he may tie, though this is not always the case. After the dog has served the bitch, if he has tied, it is best to go into the run, and for the owner of the bitch to hold her head, soothing her, whilst the owner of the dog does likewise.

The dogs at this point will be standing normally, tail to tail, with the dog's penis passing between his hind legs and into the bitch. Do not, under any circumstances, be tempted either to prise them apart, or allow the bitch to pull. Keep the dogs together, and quiet, and remain with them holding their heads until finally the dog comes free of his own accord.

At this point in the procedure, the uninitiated who have not actually witnessed the procedure before, may get a bit of a surprise. The dog's penis may appear as though something has gone wrong; the large, red, swollen, semi-erect appendage appearing unable to retract. This is entirely natural, and no attempt must be made to assist the dog. If the condition prevails then obviously the advice of a vet should be sought, but that is most unlikely. The chances of conception are obviously enhanced if another service can be arranged for the following day.

If you are using a young and inexperienced dog to perform the service, he may, in his enthusiasm, continually try to mount the bitch without actually penetrating. In this case, the best course of action is to take his penis and guide it into the vulva. Otherwise the dog may ejaculate uselessly before entering the bitch.

THE PREGNANCY

At first there may be no apparent sign of your bitch having conceived, though inside her during the first three weeks, the embryos will have fully developed. It is over the next six weeks that the puppies start to grow in the uterus, and you will see the dog starting to show physical signs that she is in pup. Her nipples and udders will start to swell. It is very important to prepare for your bitch and that you pay particular attention to her treatment and condition during pregnancy. From conception, which you should mark in your calendar, the puppies will be carried for sixty-three days, although they may be born two or three days either side of the sixty-third day.

Since she will carry puppies for nine weeks, it is important that you should increase her food for the first four-and-a-half weeks, then during the second term of four-and-a-half weeks, step up her food yet again. Do not however, simply resort to giving her an extra scoopful of food at normal evening meal times. Just like yourself it is ill advised for her to eat one enormous meal. It is preferable to start to feed her a morning meal, in addition to the evening meal, and in the second half of her pregnancy you can include a mid-day snack. In other words, you stretch the consumption of food over a longer period of time so that you prevent her from over-eating at any one meal.

Remember the motto for all puppies: what you put into their formative months is what you will get out later in life. This means in bones and muscles which starts before the puppies are born.

The growing puppies are going to make enormous demands on the bitch's system drawing all the necessary meals from the bitch. Therefore, it is essential that you step up the quality of the food you give her. It is essential that you place great emphasis on her intake of proteins, and this is best effected by making sure that she has plenty of meat and fish, and of course allow her to drink plenty of milk. In addition, take the advice of your vet who will supply mineral supplements which will provide her with all the trace elements that she needs. Of equal importance to her food is her exercise. You must prevent her from becoming fat and sluggish. If you allow her to become lazy, and do not ensure that she has plenty of exercise, then she is more likely to encounter difficulties in the later stages of pregnancy.

At this time she will start to slow down, and it would be silly to expect her to still rush about as she may have done previously. You can still exercise her but let her pace herself. Watch her general condition. If her back starts to really broaden, you may be over-feeding her, but don't drastically cut down her food, rather feed her slightly less, as you watch her condition.

Carefully plan for the time you expect your bitch to give birth. If she is kept in a kennel, make sure that it is absolutely draught free, warm and dry, and if possible fit an infra-red lamp, suspended not less than a metre above the nest. If your bitch is in the house then you are well advised to prepare carefully for the event. A stout cardboard box, well-lined with good, thick, warm, bedding material – an old blanket is ideal – is suitable. Better than a cardboard box is an old drawer, the deeper the better, since high sides are desirable to prevent the puppies waddling out and also give the bitch a feeling of security.

Try to encourage the bitch to use the box as a bed, which you should have placed in a quiet, darkened area. Most bitches will show signs that the birth of the puppies is imminent. In the last few days before their arrival she will become much more broody and will constantly scratch up her bedding in an attempt to make it more comfortable. Then about twenty-four hours before the pups are due, she will normally go off her food. It is advisable, when whelping actually begins, to have plenty of newspapers under your bitch, as bedding. Telephone your vet, inform him that the birth is imminent and enquire how you can contact him if anything goes wrong.

You will see the bitch's stomach starting to contract as she alternates the pushing and straining to give birth, punctuated by periods of rest. When the pups start to appear, do not interfere. Keep yourself and the family quiet, and allow the bitch to do what she is infinitely more competent at doing than you. As each puppy is born, she will eat the placenta, licking the puppy until it is clean and dry. The placenta is highly nutritious, but if your bitch has more than five pups, do not let her continue to eat the placentas since they may cause diarrhoea.

The advantage of using newspapers under the bitch will be seen as each puppy is born. Blood and fluid will be passed as each puppy comes out. The newspapers can be gently removed after each puppy is born, so that each subsequent one arrives on clean, dry paper.

The timing of the puppies' arrival can range from every half hour to two hours so do not be alarmed at any delay. As each puppy is born it will be encased in a thin membrane which the bitch will wash off and eat. This is the only area where you may be called on to assist the bitch. When she is freeing the membrane, if she does not manage to get it from around the puppy's head, then you may gently peel it off. Apart from this small assistance, do not interfere with your bitch unless it is obvious something is going wrong.

If, for instance the puppies are born very quickly, one after the other, she may not have sufficient time to get each puppy cleaned and dry. You can allow yourself to assist her by taking a clean, dry, soft towel, and very gently drying any puppy she has overlooked. If the umbilical cord is still attached nip it with your fingernails rather than cut it with scissors. It should be nipped off about 5cm from the puppy's tummy. If you have to do this however, take extreme care that on no account do you give any pulling pressure on the cord, otherwise you may irretrievably damage the puppy's stomach muscles.

In the majority of cases, puppies are born without undue drama. However, watch your bitch carefully. If she is still contracting and giving signs that she is still trying to push out another puppy after a period of about two-and-a-half hours then it is time to summon your vet. Lastly, if during the delivery of the pups there is a foul-smelling discharge, bile-like in consistency and green in colour get your vet immediately.

Finally, a word of comfort. Having puppies may be a big event in your home, but it is only natural to the bitch, and she is entirely capable of carrying off the whole process trouble free. Purely as an insurance it is good if you are there to gently soothe and comfort her and if absolutely necessary, lend a hand.

THE NEW PUPPIES

The new puppies will need nothing that cannot be provided by the bitch. She will provide them with food, warmth and security in the first few weeks. You need only keep their bedding clean, and make sure that the environment in which they are kept is warm, dry and draught free. It is the bitch you must pay attention to, making sure that you keep her on a high quality protein diet of fish, meat, and plenty of milk. Use the same feeding technique as you did before she had whelped, feeding her two or three times a day.

After about three weeks you should start to feed the puppies supplementary food – two small meals a day consisting of milk and light cereals. Human baby food is ideal. If you approach your local chemist he may be prepared to sell you out of date babyfood at a cheaper price.

Puppies must be taught to lap. Gently take a puppy and dip its mouth into a saucer of lukewarm milk. This compels them to lick their muzzles and, having discovered the pleasant taste, they will soon start to lap. You can also encourage them to use their tongues by dipping your finger in the milk and allowing them to lick it off.

Gradually, between the ages of three to six weeks, increase the number of meals you feed your puppies, until they are having six meals a day. When they are five weeks old, you can start adding a little meat, preferably cooked, but make sure that there is little or no fat included. You can also lightly boil fish in milk, but make sure that you remove all the bones.

Feed the puppies a little but often. If you try to feed either your bitch or her puppies on the cheap then, you will not get the best results.

As the puppies are weaned on to solid meals, the bitch's milk will start to dry up, so that by the age of seven or eight weeks the puppies should be completely weaned from their mother. At this stage, discourage any puppies that persist in trying to suckle her, and once suckling ceases the bitch's lactation will stop.

Once your bitch is free from feeding the pups you can start a gentle fitness campaign, slowly building up the amount of exercise you give her. The exercise, combined with the natural elasticity of her muscles will start to tighten her tummy, and she should, with a little help from you, regain her former shape and condition fairly quickly.

DEW CLAW REMOVAL

This simple operation must be carried out by your vet, and is normally done between three to five days old. These little rudimentary thumbs which most puppies are born with serve no useful function and it is best to remove them. They can be troublesome in later years, particularly with some breeds of dog where they are fairly prominent, and can be damaged while working in cover. Also, since they are never in contact with the ground, they can require paring to prevent them from growing into the dog's leg.

TAIL DOCKING

In the main, the practice of tail docking is largely unnecessary, being more a human fashion than of any true merit. It is claimed, by those who advocate the practice, that it prevents injury, and with some breeds, under some extreme circumstances, this may be the case. It is largely a personal choice, which you must make, and certainly potential buyers of puppies of breeds that are expected to be docked may be less enthusiastic about buying a puppy with an undocked tail.

In addition, Kennel Club standards do require tails to be docked. In the case of the GSP, between $\frac{2}{5}$ and $\frac{1}{2}$ of its tail should be docked; the springer not more than $\frac{1}{3}$, yet with the weimaraner, docking should leave only sufficient tail to cover the scrotum of dogs or the vulva of bitches. So before you embark on any tail docking exercise, look at the standard of the breed at the beginning of this book and dock to the correct length. You are best advised to take the pups to the vet. However, some vets refuse to carry out this operation since it is regarded as mutilation.

If you decide to dock the tails yourself then you must do so when the puppies are four days old. Use either a heavy carving knife or kitchen cleaver, which must be extremely sharp, and heat the cutting edge until it is hot enough to singe newspaper. Enlisting assistance, ask the person to hold the puppy on a table, with its tail laid on a flat carving board. Place the tip of the blade on the board, and in one sharp, single movement, draw the blade down through the joint in the tail. The very hot metal will of course cauterise the small blood vessels and stop the bleeding. If the tail continues to bleed, another touch with the hot metal should seal the wound. Be certain to reheat the blade before docking each puppy, and be positive in your tail docking action.

WORMING

It will be necessary for you to worm your puppies when they reach the age of four weeks. All puppies are born with worms and it is necessary for you to ensure their removal. Go to your vet for these treatments.

CLAW TRIMMING

By the time the puppies have reached four weeks they will have developed needle sharp points to their claws, which can badly scratch the bitch's stomach as they pummel her when feeding. If you see that your bitch is being caused discomfort then you should trim the puppies' claws. However, be extremely careful. Only the very tip should be removed. With dogs with pale or white claws this is easy – you can see the tiny pink core inside each tiny claw. On no account must this be cut.

SELLING THE PUPPIES

If you have a good gundog, and have gone to the trouble of having the puppies sired by a top class dog, you may find that your puppies are sold before they are born. Certainly by passing the word amongst your shooting friends you can sometimes get rid of them before eight weeks, which is the earliest they should be taken from their mother. If you are not fortunate enough to have sold them in this way, then place your advertisements in the shooting press as soon as they are born.

Your responsibility does not end merely by selling the puppies. You have a duty to try to ensure that each one is going to a good, knowledgeable shooting home, or at least to the sort of home where you think the dog will be well cared for. Ensure that you get sufficient pedigree forms well in advance (from pet shops or vets) and write one out by hand for each puppy which you must sign before handing it over to the puppy's new owner, when he collects the puppy. Take a note of who has bought each puppy as it is often useful to keep in touch with the progress of your pups. And most important, irrespective of how insistent the new buyers of your puppies are, it is essential that you spread the removal of the puppies from your bitch at least over several days and preferably over two weeks. If all the puppies disappear too quickly it can be very traumatic for the bitch, causing her unnecessary distress and confusion.

11. THE YEARS TO COME

Whilst the period of intense training which covers the first two years of your dog's life will eventually come to an end, and whilst you can relax and regard your dog as trained, you cannot afford ever to assume that all your hard work will last forever. Your dog will never forget all his training but he can slide back and become slack and sloppy if you do not keep working at giving him regular little training refreshers. Try to get into the habit, if you take him for a walk, of giving him the commands and having the same attitude to him as you would if you were

Pair of black labradors.

Above A dirty springer spaniel with too much feather before clipping
and *below* after a judicious trim the dog looks and feels better.

on a training exercise. Never allow your dog to run free, for throughout his life you must remember that irrespective of how well trained he is, if he is running free and out of your control then he is doing his own thing and this will quickly encourage him to slacken.

Many people ask the question: can a gundog be a house dog and a family pet? Of course he can. As he gains experience and mellows with age, he will become adept at recognising your moods, and as long as he always has his discipline and control kept sharp and as long as you yourself never fall for the temptation of giving him nothing to do from the end of one shooting season to the beginning of the next then he will easily cope with the dual role of working dog and pet. In fact you will gain infinitely greater reward from your dog as you get to know him as a character and personality and as the unique bond between you strengthens.

Excellent examples of this are easily seen. When my own daughters were small they used to cause great amusement by raising their arms in the air exactly as they had seen me doing and, commanding dogs large enough to look them in the eye to sit. To watch the dog, an expectant look on his face and his tail wagging, no one could doubt that he fully realised that this was a small child and they were playing a game together.

I was once on a camping holiday in a large multi-roomed tent, and my children thought it was great fun to have the two dogs lie flat on their backs between their beds. The dogs put up with a great deal of gentle child abuse and would lie where the children expected them to for all the world like large black teddy bears, albeit that they kept one eye on me for approval. Yet these two dogs, the same dogs that will gambol with tennis balls, retrieve sticks from the sea and generally behave like perfect house pets, are in fact highly skilled, impeccably mannered gundogs.

Your dog asks little of you in return for lifelong hard work and friendship, and with a little consideration, kindness and good food, will give you all his loyalty and love – a relationship which is highly rewarding.

12 EQUIPMENT AND KENNEL DESIGN

WHISTLE

A simple buffalo horn whistle will suffice. Avoid the multiple pitch or silent whistles since you cannot hear and duplicate the pitch to your own ear.

DUMMIES

It is best to spend the few pounds required on a good comprehensive set of dummies, two of the light canvas ones, and one of the heavier variety, which would simulate a heavy retrieve, such as a hare or goose. It is however permissible to make up your own dummies with washing-up liquid containers filled with sand to the weight you require and well-padded with old socks or rags firmly bound.

BLANK FIRING STARTING PISTOL

Available from most gun and sports shops. The blank firing pistol should be one with a magazine that takes several blanks, rather than one which requires re-loading after every shot.

DUMMY LAUNCHER

Invaluable, a most necessary piece of equipment and available from all good gunshops.

DUMMY LAUNCHER DUMMIES

Three are ideal – a black and a white so that you can avoid the simple confusion of knowing which one you may have lost, and a round bouncing ball to simulate ground game.

LEADS

The best lead should be made of either rope or leather and of the simple design with a loop at one end. Avoid collars, choke chains and other paraphernalia.

KENNEL DESIGN

The kennel design in the illustration is a typical good quality

Kennel design.

kennel and run, but it may be that you have either more or less ground available for this facility. The important criterion is that the box or kennel area where the dog will sleep must be entirely draught-free. This is best achieved by the entrance being low and to one side and the bed areas being raised above the floor. The kennel must either have a door, or some way of allowing you easy access inside the kennel so that you can keep it clean and change the bedding. The bedding should be changed frequently and can be a piece of carpet, an old blanket, or clean, dry straw. Avoid letting your dog lie on bare boards for long periods of time. It is less comfortable and will encourage callouses on his pressure points, such as his elbows.

The kennel run should be as spacious as possible, and whilst continually changing grass runs would be kinder, they are impractical. Therefore a concrete base is best, easily cleaned and disinfected. The whole idea of a kennel, whether you construct it in a small corner of a semi-detached garden or you have unlimited space, is that it should be dry, draught-free and warm, and that you can clean and disinfect it easily and quickly. It is also important that a dog should be able to see out of its run. Some dogs, particularly young animals, will persist in chewing virtually every corner of their kennel. This is caused by boredom or frustration and can be avoided by giving the dog a very large bone to chew.